P9-DTC-562

This is a book about submission, and it isn't what you think. It's about true submission and wholeness. It's a book about the value of women . . . and of men, too. It's about walking with Him with freedom and joy. It's not about walking the way they've told you to walk. Brenda Waggoner will make you think (she always does that), but this book could transform how you think about the issue of submission. You will thank me for recommending it.

>   **—STEVE BROWN, author, professor, and radio teacher on**
>   **KEY LIFE**

With wisdom and gentleness, Brenda Waggoner explores the often misunderstood and emotion-fraught theology of Christian submission. Always pointing to Christ, she encourages women to live an authentic life, a confident life, knowing we're in the hands of a loving, sovereign God. This is a book I'll treasure, a book I will turn to often.

>   **—JAN WINEBRENNER, author of INTIMATE FAITH**

Let my "Amen!" join the chorus of those faith-filled women who read Brenda Waggoner's book and find the welcome scent of freedom to become all the Lord calls us to be. I applaud Brenda's courage and transparency, always a fresh taste of biblical reality.

>   **—VIRELLE KIDDER, conference speaker and author of**
>   **DONKEYS STILL TALK**

What Readers Are Saying
about Brenda Waggoner's Books

This type of book is my favorite: how to live the Christian life with authenticity, taking into account how *real* life is. . . . I keep my sticky notes close at hand to mark excerpts that I want to write down or reread. This book looks like a porcupine!

—Elk Grove Village, Illinois

I just finished reading *Fairy Tale Faith*—again! It is a treasure box full of jewels of timeless truths that will not change no matter how one's personal, political, or social climate may change. [Brenda] has shown how God can take the lumps of coal in our life and through great pressures and hardships, turn those dark, unwanted experiences into diamonds.

—Alberta, Canada

I thought I would just glance through the book. . . . My glance led to a return to the first page, where I started reading. Soon I got my highlighter out and started marking what really had meaning for me. Then I started writing my own notes in the margins . . . and later found myself staring into space as I began to ponder what [Brenda] was saying to me. . . . I thought I would read this book quickly. I didn't. I read, I savored . . . I reflected, I made myself promises . . . and I prayed. . . . I received the book as a gift and will be giving it to others as a gift. I have to share this treasure with others.

—Mesquite, Texas

the *myth* of the submissive Christian woman

Walking with God
without Being Stepped On by Others

Brenda Waggoner

TYNDALE HOUSE PUBLISHERS, INC. WHEATON, ILLINOIS

Visit Tyndale's exciting Web site at www.tyndale.com

TYNDALE is a registered trademark of Tyndale House Publishers, Inc.

Tyndale's quill logo is a trademark of Tyndale House Publishers, Inc.

The Myth of the Submissive Christian Woman

Copyright © 2004 by Brenda Waggoner. All rights reserved.

Cover photo copyright © 2004 by Brian McDonald. All rights reserved.

Author photos copyright © 2002 by Joy Allen Photography. All rights reserved.

Designed by Beth Sparkman

Edited by Susan Taylor

Published in association with the literary agency of Alive Communications, Inc., 7680 Goddard Street, Suite 200, Colorado Springs, CO 80920.

The poem on pages 90–91 is copyrighted © 1985 by Brenda Waggoner. All rights reserved.

"Transcending a Problem in Christ's Strength" by Iris Pearce on pages 121–122 has been modified from the original and is used with permission.

"Marks of a Woman Living as Her True Self for the Glory of God" by Iris Pearce on pages 182–183 has been modified from the original and is used with permission.

Some of the anecdotal illustrations in this book are true and are included with the permission of the person(s) involved. All other stories are composites of real situations with names, places, and details changed to protect confidentiality.

Unless otherwise indicated, all Scripture quotations are taken from the Holy Bible, New International Version®. NIV®. Copyright © 1973, 1978, 1984 by International Bible Society. Used by permission of Zondervan Publishing House. All rights reserved.

Scripture quotations marked NLT are taken from the Holy Bible, New Living Translation, copyright © 1996. Used by permission of Tyndale House Publishers, Inc., Wheaton, Illinois 60189. All rights reserved.

Scripture quotations marked "NKJV" are taken from the New King James Version. Copyright © 1979, 1980, 1982, 1991 by Thomas Nelson, Inc. Used by permission. All rights reserved.

Scripture quotations marked The Message are taken from The Message. Copyright © 1993, 1994, 1995, 1996 by Eugene H. Peterson. Used by permission of NavPress Publishing Group. All rights reserved.

Library of Congress Cataloging-in-Publication Data

Waggoner, Brenda.
    The myth of the submissive Christian woman / Brenda Waggoner.
        p. cm.
    Includes bibliographical references (p. 187).
    ISBN 0-8423-7114-1 (sc)
    1. Women—Religious aspects—Christianity.   2. Christian women—Religious life.   I. Title.
BT704.W34 2004
248.8'43—dc22   200419074

Printed in the United States of America

10   09   08   07   06   05   04
7   6   5   4   3   2   1

*With love to my mother, Aldredge,
who gave me my first glimpse of
womanhood.*

• •

*This book is for the poor in spirit
who do not know they are blessed. It is for
those who hunger and thirst for righteousness, who long to practice biblical
submission but are confused about
what that means. It is for all who long
to become strengthened by Christ in
their inner woman. It is written as an
encouragement to keep going.*

The pursuit of God will embrace the labor of bringing our total personality into conformity to His. And this not judicially, but actually. I do not here refer to the act of justification by faith in Christ. I speak of a voluntary exalting of God to His proper station over us and a willing surrender of our whole being to the place of worshipful submission which the Creator-creature circumstance makes proper.

A. W. Tozer, *The Pursuit of God*

CONTENTS

ACKNOWLEDGMENTS

My deepest gratitude goes to my heavenly Father, for gently exposing myths in my own life and for restoring hope through submission to Christ above all others.

Thanks to my husband, Frank, for perseverance, love, and his commitment to our Lord.

Thank you to my family for sharing with me the joy of our imperfect, blessed life.

I am very grateful to Iris Pearce for all she has taught me about God's truth, love, and goodness. Special thanks to her for permission to use her exercises, which are included in the discussion and reflection sections at the end of each chapter, as noted.

Thanks to the women who shared their stories with me—at retreats, as friends, as clients. I pictured their faces as I wrote this book. Their desire to live truthfully for Christ in the midst of confusion and disillusionment deepened my conviction that God wants to expose false patterns and myths that deceptively lead his children away from his heart.

Sincere thanks to Kathy Helmers for help in conceptualizing and titling this book.

Sue Taylor at Tyndale House Publishers has done a great deal of work to make the text ready for publication. Thanks to Sue for excellent help in editing this project.

Thank you to Dr. Linda Gotts and Jan Winebrenner for help in editing and shaping this book.

Thanks also to Karen Watson, Carol Traver, and others at Tyndale who helped in the publishing process.

INTRODUCTION

*A*re mistaken beliefs about submission and what it means to "die to self" hindering you from walking authentically with God? Sometimes it's hard to tell. As Christian women, when we greet each other in public or at church, we may be all smiles on the outside. But inside, each of us is a collection of various experiences that have layered our personal histories year upon year. Most of us have enjoyed at least some good times. Many have endured seasons of physical difficulty, and some have been pelted by seemingly endless emotional storms. Although our inner state of being does not affect our significance or value in God's eyes, it greatly affects the way we view ourselves and others, the way we approach God and perceive his Word. The character of God does not change. The truths in the Bible do not change. But the experiences of our lives may cause us to perceive them differently from the way others do.

One Sunday morning during the sermon, the pastor quoted a Bible verse within the context of becoming living sacrifices for God: "Do not think of yourself more highly than you ought, but rather think of yourself with sober judgment, in accordance with the measure of faith God has given you" (Romans 12:3). The pastor concluded with another verse further down in the same text: "Be devoted to one another in brotherly love. Honor one another above yourselves" (Romans 12:10). I glanced at the faces of the women. They were listening intently. Some were taking notes and under-lining the verses in their Bibles. As I was thinking of the women listening to this practical application on how to make Jesus Lord of all, I guessed that some would be genuinely motivated by this sermon to live sacrificially. They might think, for example, *Yes, I need to remember that while I'm good at planning social events, others may have good ideas too. I'll try to be more open to their ideas.*

Other women listening to the sermon would become discour-aged as they recalled times when they had tried to apply these biblical principles to their lives. Their thoughts would run more along this line: *I shouldn't have said no when my neighbor asked me to babysit tomorrow. It's true, I'm exhausted, but I should think more highly of her needs than my own. I think I'd better call her back and tell her I'll do it.* These women would respond to the sermon by becoming self-critical or self-condemning as they decide to ignore their own needs and priorities and believe this is biblical submis-sion. The Bible was not condemning these women. The sermon was not condemning them, and God was not condemning them. Instead, *their own hearts were condemning them.* These women were not thinking of themselves with sober (honest) judgment, as the apostle Paul suggested in Romans 12:3. They were not living truthfully in submission to Christ above all others. They have bought into a myth about submission.

Traditionally, *a myth is a story that contains an element of truth and reveals a problem, a pattern, or a set of symptoms.* For example, the mythical character Narcissus became so captivated by his own reflection in the water that he fell in love with himself. He took great pleasure in watching himself smile proudly and flex his muscles, and his preoccupation with his own image eventually caused his death. Today we call this pattern of self-love narcissism.

Unlike a myth, biblical truth not only reveals a problem, a pattern, or a set of symptoms but also tells us how we can rise above the problem and become victorious. We gain the power to do this as we ground ourselves in the truth of God's Word and practice true biblical submission by embracing what God gives to us, offering it back to him, and passing it on to others around us under God's direction.

You may be wondering why I'm making such a big deal about the difference between truth and myth. You may be like my friend Linda, who learned the truths of the Bible as a child and grew up in a Christian home with a fairly healthy family. She married a Christian man and had children, and their extended family spends their vacations together. Most of their relatives go to church and have similar values. They enjoy the kind of warm, loving Christian family life we'd all like to have.

If this has been your experience, your life demonstrates God's grace and encourages others who may struggle more than you do. But even if you have not had the experiences of some women I will discuss in this book, all of us are affected to some degree by subtle misperceptions about submission and dying to self that make their way into our thinking in this fallen world. They are part of our culture—even (or perhaps, especially) our Christian culture.

My life is different from Linda's. It took me a long time to realize that I had developed some distorted perceptions about biblical submission, and a skewed picture of what it looks like to walk authentically with God. When I finally got serious with him about facing some hard truths about issues in my life, I realized it would cost a lot to give up the myths I had been living by unaware. But I wanted to grow spiritually and serve God—and that required that I learn to distinguish his truth from myths I had been believing.

When I first began my growth journey, I had no idea of the

twists and turns that lay ahead or of the gifts God would be allowing me to share today. Looking back, I must not have even known there was a difference between myth and truth because everything I was hearing sounded so "Christian." It wasn't—but we'll get to that later in the book.

Many women are unable to live in the freedom that Christ gives them to be what he created them to be because they have mistaken perceptions about what biblical submission looks like. Their struggles and concerns often go unaddressed because women don't know how to talk about them. They deny their problems in the hope that they will go away. They hide their pain because they think good Christians should "get over it," but they don't know how. In their attempts to be submissive, they unknowingly submit to other authority figures above God himself. Their behavior is mistakenly "Christianized"—it appears biblical on the outside, but internally these women are living a false, empty version of the purpose-filled, fruitful life God has planned for them.

In writing *The Myth of the Submissive Christian Woman*, I want to encourage women to embrace the gifts God has given them, to find their life purpose, and to serve Christ above all others. In each chapter, I discuss subtle counterfeits of biblical submission that often lure sincere Christian women off track in their efforts to die to self. These counterfeits, or "mythical" versions, of biblical submission may *seem* authentic on the outside. But when we take a closer look (especially at the inner workings of women's hearts), we discover that misperceptions about what God's Word teaches have caused some women to numb their hearts to their own needs, to doubt themselves, and to distort their proper priorities.

Instead of living the truth that sets them free, these woman often find that their efforts to be what they mistakenly believe is submissive lead to resentment, unhealthy relationships, and disillusionment about the Christian faith—even though they may have a lot of biblical knowledge. Unaware, these women begin living a devalued, diminished version of the abundant life God has invited them to live. Many have lost their sense of self-respect and giftedness. Ironically, the sacrifices they make often seem biblically correct. But subtle distortions of the truth bind these women's hearts and actually hold them back from serving Christ above everything and everyone else.

This is not a book about submission in marriage exclusively, although marriages are often affected by mistaken beliefs about what the Scriptures teach about submission. This is also not a "Who Am I" book, although learning to submit to God biblically will lead you to discover a lot about who you are. Instead, I want to encourage women to live truthfully and in freedom as they offer themselves to God as living sacrifices.

Each chapter begins with a "myth statement" that expresses one of the misperceptions of what it means for a woman to be submissive. You may or may not see yourself in all of these, but as you read each chapter, ask the Holy Spirit to show you if you have bought into a particular myth unaware and need to understand the truth about biblical submission.

At the end of each chapter I have included questions for reflection, discussion, and further prayer. You may use these for personal study or work through them in a small group. There is also a crystallized truth for you to take with you, to hold in your heart as you go about your days in the world. To persevere in this fallen world, you must know the truth—that Jesus Christ is your Savior and Lord of your life, that you belong to him, and that through him you are connected to your heavenly Father. These final "truths" will help you to remember that your worth is what God says it is, that it is not affected by what others say or by what happens to you, or by what you accomplish or don't accomplish.

As we learn to submit ourselves to God and grow in grace as his women, he teaches us what he has sent us into the world to do and who we are to become. He transforms our hearts, minds, and wills and gradually gives us the strength we need to die to desires that run contrary to his will. By his grace, we focus on living for Christ as our highest aim and become increasingly self-offering and self-forgetting in our service to him and to others. We may not look any different when people see us at church on Sunday mornings. But our hearts will be growing in gratitude, in freedom, in honesty in our relationships, and in deeper intimacy with God.

PART
ONE

Exposing
the
Myths

The truth is, some are afraid to learn what
lies deeper within . . . for they know He
is a Sovereign power and, if once they
catch sight of Him, He will command
their full allegiance. And then their own
will—their very self—must be changed to
become one with His.

Teresa of Avila[1]

Have You Lost Yourself?

I did not lose myself all at once. I rubbed out my face over the years washing away my pain, the same way carvings on stone are worn down by water. —Amy Tan[1]

THE MYTH: Biblical submission requires that I give up being "me."

When I first saw Nicki, she was at least fifteen pounds underweight. Her face was drawn and pale, etched with lines of pain, worry, and regret. She reminded me of a wounded sparrow in search of a sheltering limb during a storm.

On her background information she had written simply: "I need help."

"What kind of help do you think you need?" I asked.

After a long pause, Nicki shrugged and said, "I'm not sure. I just know that my life is not working."

As we began to talk, I learned that Nicki had taken disability leave from her job in an insurance company, where stress had been mounting for several years. Throughout the ten years she had worked at the company, she had received regular promotions, but recently the need to cope with her teenage son's rebellion, her husband's lack of emotional involvement in their family life and his frequent business trips, and her own responsibilities at home and work had driven her to the edge of an emotional cliff.

"I feel so guilty," Nicki said. "I've been a Christian most of my life, yet I've become incompetent in my job, and I'm failing as a wife and mother. I hate myself!" At that point the intensity of Nicki's emotions reached a peak, and she began to cry softly. Over the next few weeks, Nicki gradually gave me a glimpse of her world and, more important, the empty state of her inner self, from which she viewed it. Like a shell-shocked Christian soldier peeking out from a foxhole to view the surrounding devastation, Nicki was beginning to suspect that she may have misread her marching orders.

Nicki's lifelong tendency to avoid conflict with her coworkers, her husband, and her friends had become stronger over the years as she tried to consider others more important than herself and develop "a gentle and quiet spirit, which is of great worth in God's sight" (1 Peter 3:4). As Nicki grew increasingly concerned that she might appear selfish, she often repressed her honest emotions and denied her own needs and limitations. When her boss became anxious about the company's future and demanded extra hours of her expertise so that the business could remain solvent, Nicki frequently worked overtime. In the meantime her husband was out of town traveling at least two days each week, which left their son with unmet needs for supervision and companionship. When her husband was at home, he was often uptight or depressed. Hoping to add a little excitement to the humdrum rhythm of their lives, he persuaded Nicki that they could rekindle their waning love life by watching triple-X-rated films together. Having a desire to please her husband—and thereby please God—Nicki agreed to do this. Later, even when she felt used and betrayed, she tried to think only good and pure and right things about her husband. She kept quiet about her emotional pain because she mistakenly believed the Scriptures taught that a married woman had no control over her own body.

Because Nicki was living according to a patchwork of Scripture verses that she had pieced together over the years, her behavior looked so Christian, so right—at least from her perspective. She had always wanted to be a woman who was generous, kind, and self-sacrificing—all good traits. But she was confused and frustrated about what that would really mean for her and how to go about becoming that kind of woman. With sincere intentions of "dying to self," Nicki subtly veered off course, and her miscalculation eventually led down a dark path to self-abandonment. In the process she became a weakened, milquetoast Christian who ignored her legitimate needs for respect, accountability, and mutuality in her relationships and made it easy for unhealthy behaviors to prevail. In her well-intentioned efforts to obey what she mistakenly believed the Scriptures teach, she rejected herself and abandoned the gifts God had given her.

Nicki had unwittingly bought into the myth that in order to submit to God, she must give up being herself. Other misconceptions had also skewed her interpretation of the Scriptures, and woven together, they perpetuated a myth about the Christian life—that "dying to self" means that a woman must be weak-willed and compliant at all costs, that she must ultimately reject who she is or somehow die on the inside in order to please God. This mistakenly "Christianized" justification for devaluing what God has created may *appear* biblical at a surface glance. But when we take a deeper look, we discover that it is not at all what the Scriptures really say or what Christ intended for us as Christians: to live in freedom and truth. It is quite the opposite of the biblical submission we see in the life of the apostle Paul. Paul was strong-willed for the sake of Christ and "weak" only in that he did not get his own way in the world.

Although culture has changed over time, the truth principle we see in Paul's life has remained the same for both men and women: Following hard after Christ makes us stronger internally and defines our purpose in life, but it will not always win us accolades with others. It was this kind of submission—*a fierce yieldedness to God*—that prompted Mary, the young virgin who became Jesus' mother, to reply, "I am the Lord's servant, and I am willing to accept whatever he wants. May everything you have said come true," when the angel told her that she would give birth to the Son of God (Luke 1:38, NLT). She would have to do some serious explaining to Joseph, her betrothed, and she would face disapproval and judgment from her peers. Accepting and submitting to God's will for her would take strength—not weakness.

Yet Mary submitted to God's will first and then found the courage to give an answer to people around her. This is the freedom the apostle Paul expresses in Galatians 2:20: "My ego is no longer central. It is no longer important that I appear righteous before you or have your good opinion, and I am no longer driven to impress God. Christ lives in me" *(The Message)*.

Like many women, Nicki missed the truth of that passage. Her ego was still central. She was still preoccupied with impressing God and "appearing righteous" to other people. If we are honest, I suspect that many of us struggle with that same preoccupation, at least to some extent. The great Christian theologian A. W. Tozer recognized this. In *The Pursuit of God* he writes of a veil in the hearts of Christians, woven of "the fine threads of the self-life, the hyphenated sins of the human spirit. They are not something we do, they are something *we are,* and therein lies both their subtlety and their power."[2]

Nicki lacked this discernment. Her naive efforts to "die to self" did not lead to self-denial as described in the Bible. Instead, they led to an underdeveloped, fragile sense of self that was sheltered and weakened by choices to avoid conflict or confrontation. Her efforts to die to self created other stubborn problems that left her feeling empty, with a shallow identity built exclusively on her roles, not on who she was as a person, despite her attempts to spiritualize that emptiness away.

I have been in Nicki's shoes. When I became a Christian in my midtwenties, after five years of marriage and the births of two sons, I felt clean and pure, as if I was getting a fresh start. I wanted to serve Christ with all my heart. I began reading the Bible, going to church, and praying every day. The Bible taught different kinds of lessons, lessons I hadn't known about, such as in giving you receive, in dying you find life, and to lead others, you serve them.

My husband must have wondered where I had disappeared to on the inside once I became a Christian. He must have wondered what had happened to my spunk and individuality as I began to abandon the characteristics of my personality in the name of biblical submission. It must have puzzled him when I stopped holding up my end of our argumentative tugs-of-war as I had done in the past. These were my fledgling attempts to "die to self."

With a sincere desire to do what I thought the Bible taught, I started trying to turn away my husband's wrath with a gentle answer, to win him without a word. But then I didn't know what to do with my anger, so I just pushed it down inside me. Once in a while it spewed out unexpectedly, which confused me and made me feel guilty. Sometimes my safety instincts clamored loudly, as if to tell me that something was not right, but I told them to quiet down. Soon I became resentful, but I didn't want to talk about any of this because I thought good Christians shouldn't feel angry, confused, or resentful. Now my husband and I didn't know how

7

to talk about our conflicts at all because they were hidden, just like my feelings.

Although my husband and I no longer shared the same lifestyle goals after I came to know Christ, I still thought that my becoming a Christian would strengthen our marriage. I believe we loved each other as best we knew how at the time. But we didn't know how to honestly face and talk about our problems, work out our differences, or accept each other. Later I found out that my husband had looked elsewhere for an intimate companion he could feel close to, and eventually he left home and filed for divorce. I was heartbroken because although I knew I had made mistakes, my deepest desire had always been to be a good Christian wife and mother.

I had tried really hard to learn and obey the Scriptures, to practice them in my marriage, to teach them to my two sons, and to serve the Lord in my church and community. The descriptions of godly relationships I read about in the Bible appeared to work for some couples I knew—the men looked like strong Christian leaders, and their wives appeared to feel secure and protected. The churches I had attended taught women to rely on their husbands for making decisions, especially final ones. I overgeneralized this teaching and assumed it meant that women should also look to their husbands for safety and protection when they needed it. I had tried to be obedient, but I needed to mature in my understanding of the Scriptures.

Searching for Answers

After my divorce I tried to discuss my confusion and spiritual disillusionment with Christian friends. Some of them stared blankly at me and said things like, "Just trust in the Lord, Brenda; everything is going to turn out fine." I got the impression that since I was a Christian, there shouldn't be a problem. But there *was* a problem. Have you ever experienced this kind of confusion, when your life may have looked like others' lives on the outside and yet you knew something different must be going on inside you? I remember wishing I could somehow peer underneath the skin and bones of other women to see if any of their souls were being plowed—as mine was—with doubts, fears, and questions about what it means to be submissive as a Christian woman.

I searched for answers, but when I didn't find any, I thought something must be wrong with me since there seemed to be such a gap between my faith and what I felt inside. I had always thought that this reality would change if I prayed hard enough and had strong enough faith, but that hadn't worked for me. No matter how much I prayed, although my life had the appearance of godliness—teaching a children's class at church, attending Bible study, praying regularly, and tithing faithfully—inside, I felt hollow and empty, as if nobody was at home anymore.

I was aware that God had given me specific gifts—being a good listener, writing poems, making crafts, and caring deeply for people, especially those who are hurting. I wanted to offer my gifts to God, my husband, the church, and the people around me.

I naively thought everyone would be glad when I used my gifts, the way God delights in seeing his children use gifts he has given to them. But when others didn't respond well to my use of my gifts, I didn't know what to do. I had not yet developed discernment about whether they were mistaken or I was. Since I didn't know what else to do, I pushed my feelings away and hoped my friends were right, that somehow everything would turn out fine.

A few years passed, and I met a man at church named Frank Waggoner, who was a solid Christian and a kindhearted, outdoorsy man. We started doing things together with our kids, and before long, we fell in love. After a year of having lots of fun together and seeking God's will for our lives, we came to believe it was his plan for us to marry. So we did. And from that point on, we lived happily ever after, right?

Well, it's true that Frank and I grew very close in heart, but after about seven years of the good life together (we've now been married twenty years), the trials started up again. This was a *Christian* marriage, yet it was still facing challenges. The tension between the two of us peaked while we were attending a small, legalistic church and I got into a dicey situation as the pastor's secretary. I will talk more about this slice of my life in chapter 4, but for now I'll just say that I needed to say some hard things, both to Frank and to the pastor, and I didn't know how. I lacked maturity, but even more than that, I was so afraid of rejection that I refused to confront issues that needed to be confronted. Instead, I remained bound by the same misunderstanding that Nicki was entangled in—that in order to submit biblically, I would have to give up being "me."

I was unaware that I had begun living as a devalued, diminished version of the person God created me to be. I failed to measure up, not only to my own perception of what a Christian woman should be, but also to what I perceived the Christian community believed I should be. I was confused because even though I was a Christian, I didn't know how to make wise choices or face hard realities or set appropriate limits—or speak the truth—especially with Christian friends. I don't mean that I spoke *dishonestly* or told lies. Rather, because I didn't know what to do when people questioned my use of my gifts or had a personal agenda for the use of my gifts, I failed to speak at all. I was devastated to find out that there was mean-spiritedness not only out in the world but also among the people in my church and in me.

Later, when I went to graduate school, I found it ironic that the ones who would talk honestly with me about life's complexities were people at a secular university. Along the way I also met some Christians who would let me talk out my confusion and ask questions. They knew that we may not have answers but it is okay to ask the questions. I began to realize that through all these trials, God was trying to teach me the same lesson I'd been stuck on for a long time: *the need to live authentically and speak truthfully.*

> He Himself gave some to be apostles, some prophets, some evangelists, and some pastors and teachers . . . that we should no longer be children, tossed to and fro and carried about with every wind of doctrine, . . . but, speaking the truth in love, may grow up in all things into Him who is the head—Christ.
>
> EPHESIANS 4:14-15, NKJV

Learning to Live with Integrity

Many years later, when I began working as a counselor, I discovered that I had not been alone in this dilemma—that other Christian women had also lost the innate awareness all of us have as children of how to live with integrity, to be who we are. This loss of integrity—living our lives as a truthful reflection of who we are—affects our relationships with friends, coworkers, people in our churches, and in our communities and our marriages. More important, it affects our relationship with God. Once I realized this, I wanted to help others as I had been helped, to show compassion as others had shown compassion to me.

I talked with other Christian women who, like me, had tried to die to self before they had an awareness of and appreciation for who God had made them to be. When these women became Christians, God accepted them just as they were and brought them into relationship with him. But when it came to growing in that relationship, they mistakenly believed that they needed to give up being the unique individuals God had made them. In their minds, that is what dying to self meant. Their lack of awareness about what Christ had to say about their value created a lot of confusion about the difference between dying to self and self-abandonment.

Like me, other women didn't understand how unreasonable it was to expect themselves to authentically submit to God without the inner strength that comes from knowing you belong to someone, that you are loved, and that there is a meaningful connection in that relationship. Those who had this awareness about their relationship with God didn't understand what was missing in those who *didn't* have it. Nobody knew what to call this conviction, but I later learned that it was a solid sense of one's *true self*—the person God knows we are.

If these women had somehow been able to look deep inside, to see a visible representation of their *true selves*, it would have been clear to them that the person God created each of them to be was someone to be honored, not rejected. Valued, not shamed. Sacrificially offered, not ignored. They would have known that God had created them to be connected to him, nurtured and empowered by him, and filled with him.

They would have known that denying yourself has nothing to do with belittling, shaming, abandoning, or hiding yourself. On the contrary, it has everything to do with accepting yourself the way God accepts you—flaws and all. It has everything to do with being responsible, making choices and decisions, submitting all that you are to God as a living sacrifice. It leads to serving others through your connection to him, in a way that transcends your self. Most of all, it has to do with telling the truth in love, as children of God, the way we did when we were small.

Embracing God's Gifts

This is a very freeing way to live—to follow this daily path of "putting on" Christ. Soon we begin to leave behind the old self, with all its constantly emerging tendencies toward sin, judgment, and self-righteousness. —Julian of Norwich[3]

When I was five or six years old, my sister, Jan, and I got Ginny dolls for Christmas. Although we opened all our other presents on Christmas Eve, there was always one special gift under the tree on Christmas morning. When I opened up my doll case and saw the brown-eyed Ginny dressed in her yellow-and-brown pineapple dress trimmed with tiny green rickrack, I was so happy. I thought she was perfect—until I saw that my sister's Ginny had blue eyes.

As Jan began playing with her doll, I felt sad and mad at the same time because I thought her blue-eyed doll was prettier than mine. When I felt hot tears spilling onto my cheeks, I ran to my bedroom. I knew that my dad had taken great care in picking out those special "Santa" gifts for my sister and me, and I did not want him to see my disappointment or my tears.

After I had flung my small body across the bed and cried for a few minutes, my dad came into my bedroom. Reluctantly, I looked up at him and saw the sadness in his face. When he saw my tears, he sat down on the bed and picked up the brown-eyed Ginny, which I'd thrown onto the floor. Looking at the doll and then at me, he asked, "What's wrong? Don't you like your doll?"

"I wanted the blue-eyed Ginny, Daddy, because she's prettier," I blurted out. He reached over and gave me a hug as I sobbed uncontrollably. Soon my tears subsided, and I looked up into my dad's face. He looked puzzled as he stared at my doll.

"But she's beautiful," he said. "She has brown eyes—like you."

13

I don't remember exactly what happened after that. What I do recall is that my brown-eyed Ginny became my favorite doll. I remember the joy in my dad's hazel eyes as he watched me play with her, rolling her hair on the tiny pink curlers that came in the case, dressing her in her white flannel robe with tiny blue flowers or in her yellow-and-brown pineapple dress.

Just as my dad took joy in seeing me play with the doll he had picked out especially for me, our heavenly Father takes delight when we embrace the gifts he has given us. And how it must sadden him when we reject our talents and throw them away because they are not the ones we want or we appreciate someone else's more than our own. Biblical dying to self does not mean that we die on the inside, give up being ourselves, or abandon the gifts God has given us. It means that we embrace our gifts and talents, offer them back to God, and then at his prompting, use them in serving others for his glory.

Dying to self does not mean that we give up being ourselves or abandon the gifts God has given us. It means that we embrace our gifts and talents, offer them back to God, and then at his prompting, use them in serving others for his glory.

We see the most poignant portrait of this truth in the life of Christ, who said, "Greater love has no one than this, that he lay down his life for his friends" (John 15:13). Jesus embraced his life, accepted the charge his Father had given to him, spoke truth to his disciples, and shared the Good News from a boat or a hillside as the crowds listened. Then, after having clearly shown himself to be the Son of God, he sacrificed his life and became the ultimate offering for sinners like you and me.

Christ's pattern is clear: Accept our charge, speak the truth, and offer ourselves as living sacrifices for God's glory. Yet how difficult it is for us as Christian women to follow Christ's pattern. It is so easy to get sidetracked and settle for living in a way that we mistakenly believe is biblical. There comes a time when we have to decide whether we will live according to a myth or live out the truth.

Choosing Truth over Myth

> By dying to what once bound us, we have been released from the law so that *we serve in the new way of the Spirit, and not in the old way of the written code.*
> ROMANS 7:6 (emphasis added)

As Nicki and I continued to meet, she began to see that she had really been living according to a myth about submission, quite unlike the biblical truths she had hoped to live. Nicki discovered ways she had mixed up dying to self with abandoning self. She had lost her ability to speak truthfully as a Christian woman. She had rejected the gifts God had given her when God wanted her to delight in those gifts and use them with joy. She began to understand that over time, she had allowed what was feminine in her to be damaged, her true self to be diminished, and contrary to what Nicki mistakenly believed, this did not please God. The sin Nicki most needed to turn away from was self-abandonment—not "selfishness."

Nicki needed to learn to submit to Christ and be strengthened by him in her inner woman, her true self, the way the apostle Paul describes: "We do not lose heart. Even though our outward man is perishing, yet the inward man is being renewed day by day" (2 Corinthians 4:16, NKJV). Nicki had a choice: She could continue on in weakness, denying her true self, or she could forge ahead as Christ strengthened and renewed her. Paul's encouraging words are precisely what Nicki needed to penetrate her fearful heart so that she could grow and live free of myths that bound her.

This choice is not easy. It involves taking responsibility—facing up to low self-esteem and the sins it has led to—and learning to think truthful thoughts. For Nicki, it involved learning to identify and express her needs and to say difficult things to her husband, statements that involved the risk of rejection, such as, "I need you, and our son needs you at home." "I am unwilling to participate in this vicarious sexual affair through pornography, and I'm hurt that you want to. I must ask that you give up this deceptive form of unfaithfulness and be accountable to a spiritual mentor so that our marriage bed can again be what God intended it to be."

Nicki would have to learn how to do uncomfortable things that she had never done before. It would require integrity—being willing to confront her husband when she felt unsafe, violated, or betrayed, instead of remaining trapped in the fear of rejection and cloaking the truth in niceness. As Nicki and I worked together, I recalled how terrified I was when I began to risk such unfamiliar behaviors as valuing my own opinions and priorities, developing my strengths, and sharing the gifts God had given me.

At first, doing those things felt wrong, as if I were behaving selfishly, unbiblically, even unsubmissively. But as I took more responsibility for living for Christ, my trust began to grow larger than my fear. I started giving myself the same respect and care I would give to a friend. The same spiritual disciplines I had once practiced in an attempt to impress God and get my prayers answered in a certain way, I now entered into for a different reason: to know God and learn to serve him by offering the gifts he had given to me.

As Nicki grew stronger on the inside, she began to discover the joy of pleasing God, and her trust in him grew greater than her fear of rejection by others. On the outside her life didn't look all that different from before. But inside, Nicki was changing. It felt terrifying and uncertain. She didn't know whether or not her marriage would survive. She knew that she was willing to fight for it, but also she knew that her husband had some choices to make as well. He felt threatened by her inner growth and her truth telling because he had never seen Nicki honestly express her own thoughts and feelings before. Nicki loved and reassured her husband in ways she could truthfully do so. But ultimately, the best she could do was trust Christ and leave the results in his hands as she practiced new ways of thinking and behaving.

> [Jesus said,] "You are the salt of the earth; but if the salt loses its flavor, how shall it be seasoned?"
>
> MATTHEW 5:13, NKJV

Accepting the Challenge

When I first began thinking about this book, I knew it would lack authenticity unless it included my husband's insights as well as my own. Frank walked with me as I struggled to recognize ways I kept getting lost in a mythic maze that led me away from an authentic life with God. He has seen some of the predicaments inherent in Christian women and puzzled over some of the problems such confusion causes for their husbands and families. Together, we discovered that not only does the myth about submission not work for women, it doesn't work for the men who love them either.

We discovered truths we never would have suspected. A man can feel emasculated or rejected when his wife tries to fit him into a stereotypical role as a Christian husband. He may long for something deeper—acceptance and respect. It was painful for me to realize this must have been part of what my first husband longed for. He made the poor choice of infidelity, but I made the poor choice of avoiding reality, of hoping and praying that things would get better and mistakenly thinking that's what it meant to be submissive.

A man may feel that he is losing control if his wife embraces her gifts and becomes stronger in her inner woman. But that same situation may also, sometimes for the first time, provide an opportunity for a man to trust Christ in new ways, to grow and become more responsible and submissive to Christ himself. A secure man will be content to submit himself and his wife to God's care. I'm very grateful that together Frank and I are learning to live more honestly and responsibly, to submit our lives to God before we submit to anyone else. With God's help, we are both growing stronger.

I know that becoming responsible as women, embracing the gifts God has given to us, and learning to live and speak truthfully can be terrifying. Accepting the challenge of authentic submission requires that we face reality and call the subtle sins in our lives by their real names. But when we reject ourselves, belittle or abandon our God-given gifts, or make anyone else's personal agenda a higher priority than our service and submission to Christ, we are guilty of idolatry and pride.

This may be a hard truth to hear. But *Christ himself* supplies the courage to live for him. *He* invites us to grow. And *he,* living inside us, is our hope of glory. When we genuinely offer ourselves to him, he sets us free. Only when we are wrapped in his priceless gift of freedom can we begin to biblically die to self.

● ● ● ● ● ● ● ● ● ● ● ● ● ●

REFLECT ON THE TRUTH

As we grow in grace, we need to spend time quietly thinking about the truths of God and cultivating a meaningful relationship with him. When we do this, our outer behavior will begin to demonstrate that we give our love and allegiance to Christ above all others because of his lavish love for us.

The following questions and exercises are intended to help you prayerfully reflect on what you have read. You might want to use a

notebook or journal for writing down your thoughts, feelings, and
prayers as you go along.

Dying to Self Does Not Mean Abandoning Self

1. Begin with prayer, asking the Holy Spirit to teach you what he
   wants you to know and do as a biblically submissive Christian
   woman.

2. Read Galatians 2:20.

3. Think about the verse you have just read: *Christ living in me.* What
   an exciting thought! Yet many Christians devalue what God has
   created within them. Because they do not have a basic understanding of how God has designed them, they mistakenly believe
   that it's selfish to develop their gifts or consider their own needs.
   What do you think about this?

4. Picture yourself standing in a long line of women. Some you
   know and admire; others you have never seen. But whether
   you know them or not, you are aware that each woman in
   that line is so valuable and precious to God that he sent his
   Son to die for her. Romans 5:8 says, "God demonstrates
   his own love for us in this: While we were still sinners, Christ
   died for us."

   As you picture yourself in that line, you realize that you, too,
   are valuable and precious to God—no more and no less precious
   than each of the others. Is it harder for you to believe that you
   are *no more* precious than the others or to believe that you are
   no less precious than they are? Romans 12:3 says, "Do not think
   of yourself more highly than you ought, but rather think of yourself with sober judgment, in accordance with the measure of
   faith God has given you." How highly *ought* you to think of yourself? Leviticus 19:18 tells us to love our neighbor as ourself. This
   means that we are to love and respect others and ourselves in

19

the same way. Thinking rightly about ourselves and others helps us live in submission to Christ without getting bogged down in spiritual pride and idolatry.

5. Read 1 John 3:18-20. Although God does not condemn those who are in Christ, sometimes *our own hearts condemn us.* When has this happened to you?

   It is impossible to die to self as the Bible describes if we are preoccupied with self: *self*-rejection, *self*-abandonment, *self*-pity, *self*-doubt. You may have bought into these spiritual-sounding myths unaware, but they are burdensome, and they distract you from living out God's purposes for your life. Recognizing this self-centeredness as sin will help you to grow and thrive instead of merely survive. What spiritual myths do you need to stop believing? Confess them to God and seek his forgiveness. God will help you to stop condemning yourself in your heart, leave those myths behind, and live in freedom.

6. Close with prayer, ending with this prayer of submission: "Lord, thank you for loving and accepting me. I turn over to you my heart, mind, body, and soul. All that I am belongs to you, through Christ, who loved me and gave himself for me. Amen."

TAKE THE TRUTH WITH YOU

Biblical submission requires that I become stronger inwardly so that my trust in Christ is greater than my fear of rejection.

2

Do Your Choices Reflect Your Commitment?

Most often what holds us back from being honest is fear.
I have discovered that glass cages may look nice, but they
are no place to live. —Sheila Walsh[1]

THE MYTH: Dying to self requires that I always put others first, even if it means compromising myself and my own needs.

I was taking a break at Braum's Ice Cream Store next to my office when I heard a mother ask her three children, "What flavor of ice cream do you want?"

"Fudge Ripple," said the biggest child.

"Chocolate," said the smallest. This was followed by silence as the mother awaited the middle child's response.

"What flavor do you want, Johnny?" No answer.

"Chocolate? Strawberry?"

"I don't know," said the child.

"Hurry and make up your mind!" said Mom as the clerk finished dipping the other cones and waited for Johnny's response.

"How about chocolate? You always like chocolate!"

"Not chocolate."

"Then what? Hurry up, Johnny. What do you want?" shouted the mother as Johnny started to cry. "If you won't choose a flavor, I guess you won't get any ice cream at all!" Johnny began to wail as Mom paid for the cones, picked him up, and walked briskly out the front door.

I watched through the window as the mother packed the children into the car. A few minutes later I heard the child's voice again. He was standing at the counter with his mother and whispered weakly, "I want strawberry." Apparently Mom had reconsidered, and the child got a second chance to choose a flavor.

There is nothing unusual about that child not being able to decide what kind of ice cream he wanted and causing some commotion. But although we may not recognize it, this scenario bears strong resemblance to everyday dilemmas women face when it comes to making choices. It can be a difficult business. What if we make the wrong choice and have regrets later? What if someone we care about gets mad at us for a decision we make?

Making choices requires discernment and willingness to take responsibility for our choices. If we are putting Christ first, our choices will reflect the priorities God wants us to have, but that doesn't mean others will like our choices or agree with them. So it's understandable that we would sometimes prefer to avoid the dilemma altogether. Some choices aren't all that critical, and we get second chances, like the child at Braum's. Other times we find out the hard way that *choosing not to choose* often leads us into a choice we didn't want to make.

Many women mistakenly believe that dying to self means ignoring their own needs, attending to everyone else's, and letting others make choices for them, even if those choices cause them to compromise themselves, their priorities, and their values. Perhaps these women fear that if they say no, they will be signaling they ↙ not really committed to the other person. But this kind of passivity is more self-compromise than it is commitment, and it inevitably leads to resentment. In fact, resentment is often a woman's inner signal that she has been ignoring an important God-given responsibility—that of making choices.

Self-Compromise, Control, and Commitment

> [Joshua said,] "Honor the Lord and serve him whole-heartedly. . . . But if you are unwilling to serve the Lord, then choose today whom you will serve."
>
> JOSHUA 24:14-15, NLT

Why would a woman relinquish her power to choose? Part of the myth about submission dictates, albeit subtly, that if we want to be faithful servants and good Christians, we should give our power away to others and just be nice. There is nothing inherently good or bad about niceness; it just needs to be genuine. And sometimes, under a Christianized guise of selflessness, it's easy to mistake good manners and niceness for godliness.

Sometimes we fear being "strong" women because that sounds too much like angry women's libbers, which is clearly not the path to biblical submission to Christ. But it can be a challenge to tell the difference between being *self-compromising, controlling,* and *committed.* A *self-compromised* woman gives up her power to make choices and is unable to take responsibility for her life. A *controlling* woman uses her power to make choices for self-centered ends. She manipulates people and circumstances to fit her own agenda. In contrast, a committed woman accepts her God-given responsibility to make choices and desires that her choices will reflect God's character to others.

23

The most exhausting thing in life, I have discovered, is being insincere. —Anne Morrow Lindbergh[2]

Fried Green Tomatoes, a movie based on a best-selling novel by Fannie Flagg, gives a humorous glimpse of a woman struggling to quit compromising herself. Evelyn Couch, played by Kathy Bates, is a well-mannered, doormat wife who makes herself pretty for her husband, Ed, predicts what he'd like to have for dinner, prepares it, and then whines, "I'm sorry," when she guesses wrong. Night after night she begs Ed for a little conversation, follows him around with a steady supply of beer as he sits mesmerized in front of the TV. Ironically, the more she cajoles and tries to satisfy her husband, the more he seems to take her for granted.

Things aren't much better for Evelyn in her friendships and extended family relationships. She is isolated, starved for emotional connection, and doesn't have a clue about how to begin making changes. She enrolls in a marriage-enrichment course but begins to doubt its effectiveness when she overhears another woman comment, "What we really need is an assertiveness class for Southern women—but that seems like a contradiction in terms." Although Evelyn is momentarily intrigued by this idea, it quickly drifts out of range in her tired, confused mind.

Then in a nursing home Evelyn finds someone willing to discuss her confusion about manners, marriage, assertiveness, and what's important to women in their relationships. As she shares her purse-full of consoling candy bars with her new friend, she confides, "I feel so useless, so powerless. I can't stop eating." I can relate. Can you?

A few days later at the grocery store Evelyn loses a parking space to two slick-looking yuppie women in a Volkswagen who come from the other direction and whip into the spot Evelyn has been waiting for. Evelyn sighs and calls, "Hey, I've been waiting for that space," to which the younger women respond, "Face it! We're younger and faster!"

At this point the emotional volcano that has been building inside Evelyn erupts. Like the mythical Icarus, who flew too close to the sun and fell into the sea when the wax on his artificial wings melted, Evelyn is ripe for a meltdown after compromising her true feelings for so long. She backs her car up, throws it into drive, and plows repeatedly into the Volkswagen as she begins to laugh out loud.

The sound of metal smashing metal sends the two young women running back to their car shouting, "What are you doing?" The camera zooms in to catch the delight spreading across Evelyn's face.

"Face it," Evelyn says coolly, "I'm older, and I have more insurance."

I still remember the soft round of applause that arose from women in the theater, followed by laughter and a few whoops and hurrahs when Evelyn smashed into the Volkswagen. Something inside us stands up and cheers when Evelyn finally gets her fill of passivity and self-compromise.

Obviously I'm not encouraging women to follow Evelyn's example. Christians are to overcome evil with good—not with rage, control, or manipulation. But if we let anger go unattended and turn into cold resentment instead of learning to set limits and ask for respect, we, too, are likely to explode in fits of rage. Sooner or later we get tired of ignoring our needs and renouncing our desires. It deflates our spirit. That's why it can be confusing and damaging for Christian women who are trying to live godly spiritual lives. In their attempt to be what they mistakenly think is biblically submissive, they end up killing what God has created to thrive: a strong woman who lives with purpose.

Often Christian women think that assertiveness and submissiveness are contradictory. But let's think about that: Isn't the real truth that Christian women *must* assert themselves in order to submit to God? A *committed* woman neither obliterates nor inflates herself. She knows that dying to self does not mean *not choosing*. She knows it does not mean being passive or helpless in the sense that she waits until others make choices on her behalf. Rather, she is helpless when it comes to controlling outcomes and carving out the destinies of others, even those she cares deeply for. A *committed* woman knows that dying to self means standing in her place as God's woman—in marriage, family, friendships, church, and community—accepting the gift of freedom to make choices. She uses her power to choose God's agenda for her life, to overcome evil with good, because she has discovered the joy of becoming a new and strong self in Christ.

When you look at your own life, would you honestly say your choices reflect your commitment to Christ? Have you had battles with control and self-compromise along the way? Have there been times when you chose *not* to choose? The real battleground for choices leading to biblical submission is always internal—with foes such as hypocrisy, pride, fear of rejection, immorality, wickedness of heart. Jesus points us back to the motives of our hearts, not to condemn us but to show us our desperate need to choose his way. Even so, there are times when we lose our way and tell people what they want to hear instead of what is true, twist the truth slightly, or tell only half of it if it fits our agendas. We end up playing subtle games.

Games Christians Play

Twenty years ago Frank and I, two "nice Christians" known for our availability to other people, sweetness of attitude, and willingness to lend a helping hand or listening ear at any time, got married.

Both of our first marriages had seen their share of conflict, and we were ready for a nice, happy time serving the Lord together. Our first five or six years of life together went along smoothly. Our marriage felt like a dream come true: We got along well, and we thought this was the ultimate success since we had both been trained to be polite, to serve others, and to see to their needs. We attended a great church. Our three sons, ages ten, twelve, and fourteen when we married, did fine in school and relationships.

But just after our middle son left for college, crises started popping up faster than we could deal with them. Those crises kept surfacing like a Bo-Bo Clown that won't stay down no matter how many times you sock it in the face. As I began to take a look at some of the interactions with my friends, coworkers, and family members, it gradually dawned on me that we were involved in playing games: sometimes telling only half of the truth or avoiding it altogether so we wouldn't hurt people's feelings. Although I didn't like admitting it, I was in the middle of some of those games. On the surface our relationships and interactions appeared Christian because the players looked so nice and the words that passed between them sounded so right. The problem was, we were being phony, and that made the games harder to recognize.

I began to realize that I did not know how to be direct and clear in my communication with other people. Not only that, I didn't even see directness and clarity as desirable attributes for a Christian woman. (Though I had read the Gospels many times, I hadn't noticed that these qualities were hallmarks in the life of Christ.)

I had always found Frank gentle, fun loving, and easygoing, and yet I mysteriously and unexpectedly found myself becoming preoccupied with *appearing* submissive, as I had in my first marriage. Since I had in Frank a husband who was sensitive and easy to influence, I became concerned that if I disagreed strongly with him I might undermine his authority. If I looked too strong, he might feel intimidated. He might appear weak or end up giving in to me, and we would be doing things backward from what the Bible taught.

What I did not realize was that my covert manipulation and control—disguised as submission—eliminated the need for Frank to call on God for inner strength in discussing issues and negotiating when we disagreed and needed a solution. This enabled both of us to remain weak for a number of years as we played our well-intentioned but mistaken Christian games. Other Christians were playing games too, but nobody talked about it.

As time passed, I began to get the picture that as I sought God's guidance, he expected me to respect what I thought, felt, and preferred, to express what I needed to, and to offer others the freedom to do the same, whether they agreed with me or not. Whether or not I saw eye to eye with another person, whether others approved of my ideas and opinions or I did theirs—all of this was secondary to the issues of integrity, mutual respect, and making the choices I thought God was directing me to make. This is what it means "to do what is right, to love mercy, and to walk humbly with your God" (Micah 6:8, NLT).

It was a surprise for me—and it may be for you as well—to learn that my growing internal strength and identity actually invited others around me to face their own insecurities as they cropped up and to grow stronger themselves if they chose to. As we center our commitment on Christ instead of becoming entangled in control and compromise, relationships become the very fabric of the Christian growth process. When we trust in Christ, he weaves together our direction, decisions, choices, and results into a beautiful pattern that pleases him. Submissiveness—offering and speaking the truth in love—is one of the essential strengthening threads in the body of Christ, for both men and women.

Test the Fruit

There is so much judgment, condemnation, and prejudice
among the "saints." There is so much frozen anger among
the people who are so concerned about avoiding "sin."

—Henri Nouwen[3]

Have you become entangled in games of control and self-
compromise in your relationships when you really intended to
commit yourself to God and die to self? It happens so subtly.
How do we discern whether we are really putting Christ first?
The simplest way I know is to "test the fruit" of your submission.
When you are sincerely offering yourself to God, the result will
be love, joy, peace, patience, kindness, goodness, faithfulness,
gentleness, and self-control—the fruit of the Holy Spirit. On the
other hand, you may be trapped in a form of unbiblical submission if your efforts toward submission result in

- bitterness, because you don't get the results you wanted;
- resentment, when someone is not there for you in the way
  you hoped;
- resentment, because you feel helpless or used by someone
  else and yet you keep silent;
- vengefulness, because you harbor a hidden desire that others
  will be punished for being mean to you;
- jealousy, because others have what you don't even though
  you have prayed *persistently* for it.

The list above is not exhaustive, but it can act as a guideline to
help you reflect on your own.

Although our grown-up games are subtle and hidden, instances
of manipulation and control were more obvious to us when we
were children. Kids are so candid. My mentor, Iris Pearce, told me

a story about her granddaughter Audrey, who with a three-year-old's wisdom discovered she could get extra Oreo cookies in her children's class at church by pouting. Audrey had watched other little girls become dissatisfied with only two cookies. When they pouted, whined loudly, or began to cry, the teacher often gave them another cookie.

"I'm going to pout, Grandma Iris," said Audrey, "because it works. I like to get extra Oreos."

Three-year-old Audrey is wise to games similar to the ones we sometimes play in our churches, families, businesses, and communities. We often choose to manipulate or control others. It's easier, all right, but it doesn't get us anywhere at all if we want to grow stronger in our relationship with Christ. Sad to say, as we grow older and more sophisticated, our power plays are more hidden, and the games we play have bigger stakes than Oreos. They are more likely to be things like sexual fidelity, a child's loyalty, or the approval of a mother-in-law. It may be much more difficult to understand what's going on in our grown-up games.

> [Jesus said,] "Blessed are those who hunger and thirst
> for righteousness, for they will be filled."
>
> MATTHEW 5:6

Several years ago I was invited to speak at a church in my mother-in-law's hometown in Florida. Frank and I had not had a vacation in a long time. Both of us had been working hard, and knowing that we needed some couple time away from home, we decided to combine business with pleasure. Frank would come with me to Florida. We would stay with his mother and visit family for the first three days while I led the women's seminar. Then Frank and I would go to a hotel on Madera Beach the last two days and nights.

For me, nothing is more renewing than hearing waves crashing against the shore, feeling white sand between my fingers, and having nothing more urgent to do than watch the seagulls and cranes. But I knew our plan might present some problems because we don't see our extended families very often. It might be hard to leave after only three days of visiting. *Perhaps it would be better to wait and have our couple getaway at another time,* I thought.

"Are you sure this is a good plan?" I asked Frank. "Will your mom and brother be okay with our leaving after three days to stay on the beach in a hotel so near their homes?"

"It's a great plan," said Frank. "We'll save the cost of another airfare we'd have to buy to go somewhere else, and three days will give us time for a good visit with them." So we confirmed our plans by phone ahead of time. Frank's mom planned a dinner with some of her friends and other relatives. My sister-in-law Lori and I planned to go to the beach one afternoon while Ben took his big brother, Frank, to meet some of his buddies.

The night before we were to leave for Madera Beach, Frank, Mom, and I sat in the living room looking at photos. As we reminisced about our visit, family stories, and old times, the subject of going to Sea World together the next day came up.

This was one of those dicey times when there are two ways to look at things. On one hand, we didn't visit often, and we were all enjoying each other's company. Maybe Frank and I should be flexible and change our plans. On the other hand, Frank and I were exhausted from our work schedules and had planned part of this trip as a vacation for just the two of us. We'd made a clear agreement, and I had been counting on the time alone with Frank. So I couldn't believe my ears when I heard Frank agree that it would be fun to go to Sea World the next morning and ask what time we should leave.

"Wait a minute," I interjected. "We planned to go to the beach in the morning." Frank looked at me, puzzled, torn between two women he loved. I knew he didn't want to hurt anybody's feelings, and I felt a little sorry for him, but not much. I had been looking forward to this trip for several months. The tension hung in the air—thick and heavy.

"We don't get to see Mom very often," Frank said. The two of them talked it over as anger rumbled inside me and threatened to erupt.

As the tension reached its pinnacle, Mom interjected, "Let's go to the Lord in prayer."

Now, I know that prayer is our lifeline to God, and I love to pray, but at that moment I gagged on the thought. Frank and I had already prayed about our plans for weeks. There was a battle raging inside me as one side accused, *Don't be so selfish!* and the other answered, *It's not selfish—it's telling the truth!* In this instant I was caught in the difficult choice between seeking the admiration of people I loved by appearing virtuous and submissive but battling resentment later or speaking what I thought was truthful and right and risking disapproval from those I loved.

Reminding myself not to whine and summoning the steadiest tone I could manage, I looked Frank in the eye and said, "Excuse me. We've already prayed about this, and so I think I will go to the beach."

A cool, tense silence filled the room.

I wasn't trying to be argumentative. I didn't want to rebel against God. I wasn't trying to avoid prayer or be unsubmissive. I just wanted us to enjoy the vacation Frank and I had agreed on, looked forward to, planned and budgeted for. It seemed to me that prayer was being used as a manipulative game. One of us got up to get a glass of water, the conversation switched to something lighter, then we had a small snack and went to bed.

The next morning Frank and Mom dropped me off at the beach, where I had a relaxing day by myself while the two of them spent the day together (although not at Sea World). I later learned that they spent the day talking. Frank had explained our priorities to Mom and his promise to spend two days at the beach with me. He ended up apologizing to her, and later to me, for doing both of us wrong by not keeping his word. That evening when the two of them picked me up at the beach, Frank brought flowers as a peace offering, along with our luggage and a hotel reservation so we could stay our last night on the beach.

Although I wish I had been less awkward in that situation, it was a fledgling step in learning to live with greater integrity—an attempt to stop compromising myself. It was also a step away from stockpiling resentment and a step toward truth telling.

As Christian women, we need to recognize and think beyond the games we may be playing and take a clear look at what's really going on inside us. Dying to self does not mean ignoring your own needs or not holding others to their word. It means wanting Christ's righteousness more than anything, even if it causes tension in your relationships. I admit that I would have preferred the two nights at the hotel with Frank—and the pleasure of his company instead of the flowers—but Frank was learning a few things too. In fact, Frank, Mom, and I were all learning a difficult lesson together about priorities, integrity, and mutual submission.

> *Dying to self does not mean ignoring your own needs or not asking others to keep their word. It means wanting Christ's righteousness more than anything, even if it causes tension in your relationships.*

Even though taking a stand for our priorities and preferences may at times be awkward, make us unpopular, or cut across cultural or family norms, we won't be able to stand in our place as God's women unless we make choices that honor him and keep us honest. So often we try to be noble and self-sacrificing, and it may look from the outside as though we are succeeding. But inside, we know we are betraying the truth within us. God has a path on which we should go, and he will lead us, one choice at a time.

●●●●●●●●●●●●●●●

REFLECT ON THE TRUTH

The following questions and exercises are intended to help you prayerfully reflect on what you have read. You might want to use a notebook or journal for writing down your thoughts, feelings, and prayers as you go along.

Self-Compromise Is Not the Same as Commitment

1. Open with prayer.

2. Read Psalm 37:5. How do you think self-compromise affects commitment to Christ? If you are using a journal, record your thoughts.

3. Read 2 Timothy 1:7. Christ has given us a spirit of power, love, and self-discipline. Have you developed these qualities? Write down your thoughts. If not, write a plan for how you will work on receiving and making use of what Christ gives to you in empowerment, love, and self-discipline. What will it look like for you to stand in your place as Christ's woman?

4. The fruit of genuine submission to God is the fruit of the Holy Spirit. Read about the fruit of the Spirit in Galatians 5:22–23.

Contrast this with the "fruit" of self-compromise and other counterfeits of submission. Write your thoughts in your journal.

5. Read through the following reflection and think about how easy
or difficult it is for you to make choices in freedom.

> *As a child of God . . .*
> *I can choose joy in this life, here and now.*
> *I can choose to relax and have fun, to offer my gifts, dance, sing,*
>   *make up a recipe, or . . .*
> *I can choose to say no when I feel something is not safe or I am*
>   *not ready.*
> *I can choose not to participate in chaotic behavior of family*
>   *or friends.*
> *I can choose to leave the company of people who lay a guilt trip*
>   *on me.*
> *I can choose to leave the company of people who manipulate and*
>   *humiliate me.*
> *I can choose to care for and respect myself. This is not selfish.*
> *I can choose the way I will think and behave and accept all my*
>   *feelings.*
> *I can feel all my feelings—they are a part of me, and God*
>   *understands.*

6. As you close in prayer, thank God for his unspeakable sacrifice in
sending Christ to die. End with the prayer of submission: "Father,
thank you for loving and accepting me. I turn over to you my
heart, mind, body, and soul. All that I am belongs to you,
through Christ, who loved me and gave himself for me. Amen."

TAKE THE TRUTH WITH YOU

Dying to self means honoring Christ above all others. As God
directs me, I will try to make choices that honor him, and I will
trust him to show me when I make mistakes so that I can correct
course and get back on track.

3

Is Your Success Formula Failing?

Our little systems have their day;
they have their day and cease to be:
they are but broken lights of thee,
and thou, O Lord, art more than they.

—Alfred, Lord Tennyson[1]

THE MYTH: Biblical submission requires that I follow a clear-cut formula for the successful Christian life. If I follow it precisely, I will earn love and approval from God and others.

"If I hear one more person mention the word *submit,* I'm going to throw something!" Cindy fumed. She and her family had recently moved from the San Francisco Bay area to a small farming community in Texas. They were having trouble adjusting to their new environment and finding ways to fit in and serve Christ as they had in their former home.

Cindy had nobody to confide in, no moms to get together with, and she was suffering from the lack of intimacy she'd once enjoyed and felt isolated. Cindy was also growing resentful because her husband was spending so much time at work and with his new friends. In an effort to find a woman she could confide in, she'd asked the leader of her women's group to come to her house for coffee. Later, Cindy described their conversation.

"It was hard to open up to someone. But I finally got up the courage to be honest. When I tried to tell her what my life is like, how alone I feel, how angry I am becoming, she responded with a pat Christian answer: Pray, go to church, submit to your husband, and die to self. In time, everything will turn out. I wanted to say, 'Knock, knock. Is anybody home in there?' I don't think she really heard one word I said!"

Cindy was angry and disappointed with the simplistic fix offered by someone she respected. She was *already* doing what the woman suggested. She was trying to rely on God's Word and prayer, to find a church to belong to, to submit to God and the other authorities in her life, so the woman's suggestions felt like putting a Band-Aid on a very deep wound and only made Cindy feel worse.

Cindy was left feeling condemned for having problems and a messy life. She was a Christian, and the Bible had all the answers, so why was she an emotional mess? Cindy now faced a choice: She could try harder to make a formula for success work, or she could move toward something more meaningful with God.

When we try our best to follow God's Word and to live in his ways and yet still encounter problems, we may assume that we are not trying hard enough or not following God's directions precisely enough. But God is up to something much bigger. He is building our character, and only he knows what that will take. As much as we don't like it, when God wants to strengthen our character, he often uses painful trials that lead us out of our comfort zones and drive us into his arms. At such times, what we need from friends is acceptance, encouragement to persevere, and someone to come alongside us and trust God with us.

38

Trying Harder Doesn't Work

> Observe how Christ loved us. His love was not
> cautious but extravagant. He didn't love in order to
> get something from us but to give everything of
> himself to us. Love like that.
>
> EPHESIANS 5:2, *THE MESSAGE*

Cindy's story is not uncommon. I've heard similar accounts from many women, and you probably have too. Her experience reminds me of a group of college seniors I heard about. Knowing that they would soon be going their separate ways, they decided to climb a mountain together just after graduation as a bonding experience. As they started up the mountain, the athletic people were leading the pack. Those who weren't as physically fit fell in behind. As the classmates worked their way up the mountain, the athletes were farther out in front, and soon they could look down the mountain and see that one overweight woman was falling behind all the others. The leaders called down to her, "Come on, you can do it! Just try harder!"

The woman called back breathlessly, "I'm trying. I'm doing my best, but I don't know if I can make it."

The leaders pulled out still farther as they called down again to the one falling farther and farther behind. "Try harder! Try harder! Come on, you can do it!"

"I'm trying, I'm trying," she called back, between huffs and puffs. The glib sentiments from those who were succeeding deflated the woman's spirit because she was already trying as hard as she could. The others were athletes, and they didn't understand how hard it was for her to just keep going.

If the athletes had really wanted to encourage the woman lagging behind, they might have gone back down the mountain

39

and tried walking alongside her *at her pace*. It would not have been an easy thing to do. They would have missed the thrill of being out in front, of reaching the top first, and it was much easier to just shout instructions at her. But it would have been a lot closer to what biblical submission really asks of us—selflessly serving a sister who is weaker at the time.

It's sad that the leader of Cindy's women's group appears to have been unwilling to really serve a weary fellow traveler when her life wasn't looking successful. Perhaps she didn't know how to offer encouragement to a discouraged sister just because she was a child of God. I have to admit that I have been on both ends of this problem, sometimes bewildered by simplistic suggestions of those who appeared strong and other times offering condescending though well-meaning solutions to others without giving them any quality attention.

I've sometimes wondered what's really going on with us as Christian women when we do this to each other. Do we tell others to try harder and offer pat answers because we don't really want to be bothered with the real needs of people? Are we in need of having others look up to us? Or do we just want the easy way out because we're so busy with our own lives? As members of the body of Christ, we need to consider the effect our simplistic solutions can have on others. Most of the time pat answers don't accomplish much more than giving a little pat on the back so we can quickly move on to "more important" things. What we may not realize is that those pat answers often leave the person who is struggling in even greater need than before.

Sooner or later we all face the choice Cindy faced: Do we cling to our formulas for successful Christian living, trying harder and harder to make them work, or do we journey with Christ on a spiritual path where we must trust him as he works in ways we would never choose to produce growth and maturity in us?

God's ultimate goal is to develop Christlike character and conform us to the image of his Son. We have no way of knowing what that will take.

Christ's Path to Fulfillment

We are actually pioneers trying to find a new path through the maze of tradition, convention and dogma.
—Anne Morrow Lindbergh[2]

In our current age, filled with seminars, workshops, books and Bible studies, multimedia resources, and small groups of all types—all good things in and of themselves—the latest ideas for how to have a successful Christian life spread like wildfire. We know enough to reject the world's path to recognition and fulfillment: money, sex, and power. But sometimes we too easily adopt a Christian success formula for approval, thinking that it will make our lives turn out right and cause us to look "out in front" in the eyes of God and our Christian peers.

Every group—whether a family, a church, or some other social unit—has unwritten codes of conduct for earning approval and defining success. You won't find these codes posted in the hallways, but they're engrained in us. Solid Christian teachings about putting others first, submitting to authorities, and being servant leaders to those in our charge often naturally earn us approval from peers, and it's great when things work that way. But sometimes what it takes to please people is not the same thing it takes to please God. In those situations we may become confused about how to submit to God above all others.

Women are especially vulnerable to this lure away from submission to God first because we are relational beings. It's especially important to us to feel close to significant people in our lives. When you add together a woman's natural desire for close-

41

ness and her efforts to be submissive to God and other authority figures in her life, is it any wonder she easily becomes confused?

For a long time I was like the leader of Cindy's group, hoping Christian success would come neatly packaged in a three-step plan—study the Bible, pray, and go to church—similar to the way brushing our teeth, washing our face, and combing our hair are steps to good personal hygiene. For a while, the formula I followed for Christian success seemed to work. I prayed, studied my Bible, and went to church, and my first marriage stayed together, my kids did fine, and I felt proud. I didn't realize it, but I wanted to take credit for the fact that things were going well. I wanted to believe that good things happened because I did things right. I thought God had blessed me because I deserved it. But the subtlety of self-righteousness blocks us from embracing God's grace, which we can never earn.

Learning the truths of Scripture, praying, becoming obedient and submissive to God, and practicing other spiritual disciplines are essential elements of the Christian life. Of course it's right to practice them. Without the practice of spiritual disciplines, we will not mature in our spiritual lives. But it's not the practices that make us holy; it is God's Holy Spirit working in us that makes us holy.

In the spiritual life, God doesn't want our success formulas to work. He doesn't want them, or anything else, to be used as a substitute for trusting him. Although gaining approval from our peers and authorities is a natural desire and feels good, it's wrong if we put it ahead of pleasing God. Most of us need some practice telling the difference between what we may call success and what is truly success on God's terms.

Learning to Trust

Jesus' formula for success leads us toward proven character and becoming stronger in our inner woman, and we don't always know what it will take to get us there. If following four or five clear-cut steps predictably resulted in proven character, there would be no need for us to trust Christ to lead us through trials. Nor would we find out how desperately we need him. The steps to Jesus' definition of success are custom tailored for each of us, and we don't have the ability to figure out ahead of time what they are. They include learning the truths of his Word, praying, and serving in a church. But they also include whatever it takes to bring about perseverance, proven character, and hope, and often it's suffering that presses us on toward hope (see Romans 5:3-4).

"Blessed are the meek, for they will inherit the earth," said Jesus in Matthew 5:5. One definition of *meekness* is "enduring injury with patience and without resentment."[3] Isn't meekness the quality it takes to persevere when life is messy and you don't understand why—when you know that even when others misunderstand you, God is somehow at work behind the scenes? Blessed are you at such times, Jesus says. Now that's comforting, and encouraging!

The way of the blessed life Jesus describes in the Beatitudes includes poverty of spirit, mourning, meekness, and hungering after righteousness. But those are not steps I hoped would lead me to success as a Christian. I didn't much like the way Jesus defined Christian perfection either. (The Greek translation of *perfect* is "to complete that for which one was created.") Only Jesus fully knows the unique purpose for which he created us, so only he can do this work of perfection in us. It's a divine setup—there's just no substitute for trusting him in a day-to-day relationship.

God operates according to an economy vastly different from ours: "As the heavens are higher than the earth, so are my ways higher than your ways and my thoughts than your thoughts," he says in Isaiah 55:9. His thoughts are incomprehensible to us. We pray, thinking we know what it will look like for our lives to be successful and blessed. Not only is that not true, but our definition of blessing is always changing. At four, blessing may mean a shiny new bike with training wheels or a plastic ball and bat. At fourteen, our idea of blessing may be a cute boyfriend. At twenty-four, blessing may be a college degree and a corporate job. At thirty-four, it's a new house in the right part of town, two cars, and a child or two in excellent health.

It would seem obvious that blessing equals a successful life as we picture it, and the way to earn that blessing is by practicing the right steps and disciplines. But if we glory in the practice of the disciplines instead of in God himself, religion becomes a performance. Our focus subtly and deceptively shifts, and instead of trusting in God, we try harder, helping God out here and there so that we can be sure life turns out the way it's supposed to. Sometimes it takes us years to learn that the blessed character and attitudes that Jesus described in Matthew 5 are unattainable by self-effort; rather, they are wrought in the Christian by the work of the indwelling Holy Spirit (see 1 Corinthians 3:16 and Galatians 5:22-23).

In my younger years as a Christian, I wandered through a maze of self-righteousness that blocked me from living in the light of God's grace. We all have mazes we wander in and out of, and they are not entirely bad; they're just misperceptions of truth. The Bible is clear, but our perceptions are distorted. These misperceptions lure us away from God's best for us. The disciplines of prayer, Bible study, and church attendance that I practiced as a young Christian were a foundational part of my Christian growth. But at some point, without realizing it, I started expecting them to earn me the life I wanted—Christian success on my own terms and blessings I could recognize,

Then one day as I was in midsentence telling God what a lousy job I thought he was doing with my life, how I had tried to do everything right, and how lonely I felt because he wasn't paying attention, he gave me a sense of his loving presence and compassion. It was as if he lifted my chin and said, *Look at me. Don't you know that I have always loved you? Don't you know that I formed your very being, and I know every detail of your life? Don't you know that I am not surprised by what is going on in your life and I have been waiting for you to simply look at me, trust me, and follow me?*

His strong, loving presence melted my heart in a way I have never yet recovered from. From that point on, although I have had other struggles and wandered in and out of other mazes of distraction, I have been convinced that my performance can never earn me what I want most—God's love and approval. There is only one way to true success as God would define it for me: to open my arms to his love and to trust in this Jesus, who is so personal, so kind, so tenderhearted, and so close by.

What mazes of distraction draw you away from God's best for you? Often they start out as good things, things you feel passionate about, such as doing good deeds for others, taking on responsibility, caring for people, or leading a righteous life. Yet in your sometimes overly diligent efforts, without really being aware of it, you somehow step over an invisible line. Caring becomes overcaring, and you end up enabling and weakening people you care about. Responsibility becomes overresponsibility. Righteousness becomes self-righteousness because it counts on its own ability to get results if you try hard enough.

Giving of our time and energy becomes overgiving as we offer to others more than we really have to give, which results in frustration and disappointment for ourself and for others. Our passions, overdone, lead us into mazes as we give them God's place, and we end up trapped. Things we thought would bring us success and approval from God and others end up defeating us because we are not really trusting him. The good news is, if we know what our mazes are, we're less likely to get lost in them.

Success on God's Terms

As Christ strengthens and renews us in our inner woman, we learn to rely more and more on him. When disappointments come or things don't turn out the way we think they should, we begin to see that somehow, in a way we cannot comprehend, God is at work on our behalf. He is sovereign and trustworthy. He is accomplishing his good purposes, even though our lives may not impress others at all. In ways we are not aware of, God is crafting within us qualities like humility and meekness, honing our character, strengthening us, and making us successes on his terms.

In ways we are not aware of, God is crafting within us qualities like humility and meekness, honing our character, strengthening us, and making us successes on his terms.

What will it look like in your life for you to submit yourself to God for an inner makeover? What changes do you need to make today so that you are trusting him to prove your character instead of relying on performance religion—pat answers and formulas for answered prayers and success according to your own definition? As we submit ourselves to God above all others and trust in him whether or not we get what we want, we become less preoccupied with our image as a Christian. Without our really being aware of it, God gradually changes us inside and makes us more like Jesus. Nothing external will ever be able to match the reward of pleasing him and trusting him to make us over for his glory.

I didn't want some petty, inferior brand of righteousness that comes from keeping a list of rules when I could get the robust kind that comes from trusting Christ—*God's* righteousness. I gave up all that inferior stuff so I could know Christ personally, experience his

resurrection power, be a partner in his suffering, and
go all the way with him to death itself.

PHILIPPIANS 3:9-10, THE MESSAGE

● ● ● ● ● ● ● ● ● ● ● ● ● ●

REFLECT ON THE TRUTH

The following questions and exercises are intended to help you
prayerfully reflect on what you have read. You might want to use a
notebook or journal for writing down your thoughts, feelings, and
prayers as you go along.

The Christian Life Is Not a Success Formula

1. Jesus described his path to success, or blessing, in the Sermon on
   the Mount (Matthew 5:3-12). His words do not always include
   the same things we would include in a formula for success. But
   his thoughts are higher than our thoughts, and his ways are not
   our ways. Matthew 5:3-5 reads this way in *The Message*: "You're
   blessed when you're at the end of your rope. With less of you,
   there is more of God and his rule. You're blessed when you feel
   you've lost what is most dear to you. Only then can you be
   embraced by the One most dear to you. You're blessed when
   you're content with just who you are—no more, no less. That's
   the moment you find yourselves proud owners of everything that
   can't be bought." Think about how different these descriptions of
   blessing are from what we may learn in the world, in our families, or in our churches.

2. Have you been lured into following success formulas in your
   Christian life? If so, in what ways? If you are using a journal,
   record your thoughts.

3. *The Inner Voice of Love* is a collection of writings by Henri Nouwen to himself at a period in his life when he suddenly lost his sense of being loved. His vulnerability and reflections may deepen our awareness that we are truly not alone in our struggle to love and be loved in healthy ways: "Part of your struggle is to set boundaries to your own love—something you have never done. You give whatever people ask of you, and when they ask for more, you give more, until you find yourself exhausted, used, and manipulated. Only when you are able to set your own boundaries will you be able to acknowledge, respect, and even be grateful for the boundaries of others."[4]

   Can you identify with these words? Do you ever struggle with setting boundaries? Write out your thoughts.

4. Read the following thoughts from Henri Nouwen: "You keep listening to those who seem to reject you. But they never speak about *you*. They speak about their own limitations. They confess their poverty in the face of your needs and desires. They simply ask for your compassion. They do not say that you are bad, ugly, or despicable. They say only that you are asking for something they cannot give and that they need to get some distance from you to survive emotionally. The sadness is that you perceive their necessary withdrawal as a rejection of you instead of as a call to return home and discover there your true belovedness."[5]

   The next time you feel rejected because someone indicates a need for distance or solitude, remember that this is an opportunity for you to be alone too—alone with God. Spend time in quietness or personal worship, or go for a walk, being mindful of the beauties of God's creation and thanking him for them. Let your feelings of rejection drive you to God's arms and to gratitude.

5. God has his own ways of making us perfect (i.e., complete). But we don't get there by practicing perfectionism. It is healthy to pursue excellence for Christ's glory, but it is not healthy to be

driven by perfectionism. Listed below are some of the differences between perfectionism and a pursuit of excellence for Christ's glory. They reveal contrasting motivations of heart. Write down your thoughts, noting particular ways you need God's help.

Perfectionism: You are motivated by fear of making mistakes, and when you do make them, you become self-critical, fearful of rejection from others and of punishment from God. You feel stressed out, driven, and your accomplishments never satisfy you. You can never do enough. You feel gratified when you impress others, and you use your accomplishments and performance to try to win love and approval from others. You are always in control of your emotions.

Pursuing Excellence for Christ's Glory: You are motivated by a desire to please God. When you make mistakes, you encourage yourself to keep going by saying, "Next time, with God's help, I will do better." You are motivated by God's love and grace. You are not afraid to be vulnerable, to share your feelings, or to ask for help when you need it. You have creative energy and enthusiasm, and you feel worthwhile because God loves you. You enjoy your accomplishments and are grateful for them because you know they are gifts from God.

6. Write a prayer of thanksgiving for God's gifts to you; then close with the prayer of submission: "Lord, thank you for loving and accepting me. I give to you my heart, mind, body, and soul. All that I am belongs to you, through Christ, who loved me and gave himself for me. Amen."

TAKE THE TRUTH WITH YOU

God is concerned with building my character and conforming me to the image of Christ. I do not know all the steps that it will take, but it will require that I trust him above all others. I will practice spiritual disciplines out of devotion to God—not in futile efforts to earn the blessings I think I should have.

4

Are You Crawling onto the Cross?

Lord Jesus, we are silly sheep who have dared to stand before
you and try to bribe you with our preposterous portfolios. . . .
Give us the grace to rely on your mercy no matter what we
may do. —Brennan Manning[1]

**THE MYTH: Biblical submission requires that I follow
precise biblical role descriptions for relationships,
even if it means ignoring my instincts about safety and
emotional well-being.**

Juliana and Marc had been married almost eight years, and many
of their friends looked up to them. But after the birth of their
second child, conflicts occurred more frequently, and they
decided to enroll in a marriage class at their church. They hoped
that a little practical training in problem solving and communication would increase their emotional intimacy.

The class began well, but soon the focus shifted from communication to a meticulous examination of Ephesians 5 and the specific
roles of husbands and wives. The leader seemed to imply that

biblical submission required husbands and wives to follow precise role descriptions. If they did, their marriage would run like a well-oiled machine. Marc and Juliana worked hard at modeling what they saw in Ephesians, but the harder they tried, the more frustrated and confused they became.

One day when Juliana and I were together, she read aloud to me from the Bible, "Wives, submit to your husbands as to the Lord. For the husband is the head of the wife as Christ is the head of the church, his body, of which he is the Savior. Now as the church submits to Christ, so also wives should submit to their husbands in everything" (Ephesians 5:22-24). Then she explained that the leader of the class had used these verses as a basis for listing traits of godly wives for the women and traits of godly husbands for the men.

"I know these role models are straight out of the Bible, and I want to follow God's guidance," said Juliana. "It almost feels like blasphemy to say this, but something doesn't seem right. Marc and I are changing, but I don't think it's for the better. We're not comfortable being ourselves anymore."

Juliana shared how her husband had begun focusing on becoming a stronger head of the household, making decisions, paying bills, disciplining the children, and becoming more attentive to his wife's emotional needs. Juliana had been concentrating more on looking to Marc for leadership. That sounds good, doesn't it? But the rub was that Marc had always respected Juliana's insights and perceptiveness and had relied on her to make many of their practical decisions, pay the bills, and discipline the kids. Now Juliana's personal strengths seemed to cut across the grain of the biblical model they had been studying.

She and Marc had hoped the class would teach communication and problem-solving skills, but instead they had discovered that their usual way of fulfilling their roles as husband and wife no longer seemed biblical. Juliana questioned whether she was submitting to Marc or failing to follow his lead if she made decisions, since according to their lists, that seemed to be his job. Yet as Juliana worked to fit into what she perceived to be the ideal mold, the praise she received from her friends made her think maybe she should continue even though what she was doing now felt phony and forced.

"Last week's meeting emphasized that as an act of Christlike love, husbands should listen attentively to their wives instead of jumping in quickly to solve the problem," Juliana said. "But Marc is carrying this too far—and he's acting weird! Now he asks me about my day the minute he gets home from work. I even found a yellow sticky note stuck to the dash of his car. On it he had scribbled, 'Ask Juliana about her day. Maintain eye contact!'" Juliana paused. "I just want us to be real with each other. Yes, we need to learn better ways to resolve our conflicts, but I just want Marc to love me!"

The rigid way Juliana and Marc were trying to make themselves fit the role descriptions on their lists was choking out their love and their sense of emotional well-being. As Juliana concentrated on submitting to Marc and waited for him to make decisions about things she had always been responsible for, Marc began to feel emasculated and unaccepted, and Juliana felt stifled and unneeded.

"What do you want from me?" Marc finally demanded in the midst of an argument. "You are expecting me to be like ——— [the leader of the class], and I'm *not* like him! Maybe what you really want is somebody else."

"What do you mean?" Juliana countered angrily. "I give, give, give, and it's never enough. I try to be unselfish and submissive, but you don't appreciate it!"

As Marc and Juliana focused on the prescribed portraits of

godliness, they became critical of each other and of themselves. There were no more kisses or caresses. They lost track of the larger goal of honoring each other as they trusted Christ and together submitted their lives to him. Their calculated efforts to follow precise role descriptions had gained them some praise from their peers, but that wasn't nearly as rewarding as an honest relationship with each other, even with all its struggles.

Like many of us, Marc and Juliana had experiences from their childhoods that influenced their interpretations of biblical ideals. There were reasons they had trouble fitting into an "ideal wife" role or an "ideal husband" role. Because Marc's single mom had raised him alone, strength and independence characterized his model of femininity. He admired Juliana's initiative, just as he'd admired his mom's. Yet the idea of healthy, strong, masculine leadership in the home was an enigma to Marc since he hadn't even known his father.

Juliana, on the other hand, had grown up in a Christian home. Her dad, a busy corporate executive, was gone a lot, so her mom ran the household. But although Juliana's dad was a good provider, he was preoccupied and emotionally absent—even when he was at home. Juliana didn't want to see this pattern repeated in her own home, so it was especially important to her that Marc spend quality time with the children.

Interestingly, as Marc and Juliana took a few steps back from their intense focus on following role descriptions and criticizing each other for falling short, they made new and deeper discoveries in the Scriptures. They noticed that in the very beginning of Ephesians 5, before the verses the class had concentrated on, were these words: "Be imitators of God, therefore, as dearly loved children and live a life of love, just as Christ loved us and gave himself up for us" (vv. 1-2). It was liberating to realize that only after the apostle Paul explained God's overall goals for the church did he go on to present the steps toward godly relationships.

The Bible describes a way of living as a husband or a wife who is drawing strength and purpose from a source: Jesus Christ. Those descriptions are not law. It's good to learn these principles, but we shouldn't use them to put Christian relationships in boxes with step-by-step directions on the side. Instead, under God's guidance, couples need to respectfully flesh out the biblical principles with sensitivity to each other's spiritual gifts, personal histories, and emotional wounds that God is in the process of healing.

Trying to Impress Others

I've often heard it said that if husbands were strong godly leaders, their wives would have no problem submitting to them. Some Christian couples enjoy such a marriage relationship, but many Christian men have not had the benefit of training about biblical masculinity. They and their wives are works in progress, growing as God heals and matures them. God gives us the gifts he wants us to have. Our responsibility is to offer those gifts back to him for his glory.

Relationships are the context in which people grow and mature. If we are to develop healthy, God-honoring relationships in which he is strengthening our inner man and inner woman, we must live with integrity and face the truth about ourselves and others. We must admit our real needs and then trust God to guide us and develop our gifts as we work toward his ideals. Otherwise, how will we kiss the graves of our imperfect parents instead of blaming them for our deficiencies? How will we pass on to our children some measure of God's blessing if we don't admit the truth about our less-than-ideal lives and grow from there?

Jesus said, "Blessed are the poor in spirit, for theirs is the kingdom of heaven" (Matthew 5:3). The poor in spirit know they need

God, that they can't make it without him. And although others may not see dependence and neediness as desirable qualities, God is pleased when we acknowledge our dependence on him. He already knows how imperfect and unfinished we are, but we have trouble admitting it. We often find it easier to trust in our own misguided sense of perfection than to admit our utter dependence on him and trust him alongside the one with whom we share our relationship.

We can only wonder how the number of successful Christian relationships might multiply if we learned to be truthful about our need for God instead of meticulous about perfecting the roles we play. The fulfillment that comes from submitting our hearts to God and offering our spiritual firstfruits for his glory far surpasses the hollow praise of others for appearing to have a model relationship.

The Lord beyond the Laws

Here also lies the fundamental mistake of the scribes and Pharisees. They focus on the actions that the law requires and make elaborate specifications of exactly what those actions are and of the manner in which they are to be done. They also generate immense social pressure to force confor- mity of action to the law as they interpret it. They are intensely self-conscious about doing the right thing and about being thought to have done the right thing. —Dallas Willard[2]

The Pharisees were notorious for trying to impress others with their holy-looking behavior, but they had no regard for people's uniqueness, needs, and circumstances. They repeatedly tried to pin Jesus down, trip him up, and catch him breaking rules. Matthew 12 shows Jesus' disciples picking grain and eating it. Of course, the Pharisees are quick to point out their error: "Look! Your disciples are doing what is unlawful on the Sabbath" (v. 2).

Do they sound a little like preschoolers looking for a chance to tattle?

Jesus reminds them that David entered the house of God when he and his companions were hungry and ate the consecrated bread, which was lawful only for the priests. Then Jesus says, "Haven't you read in the Law that on the Sabbath the priests in the temple desecrate the day and yet are innocent?" (v. 5). In other words, the priests' Sabbath work, necessitated by the sacrificial system, was acceptable.

Of course Jesus knew that it was important to keep the Sabbath, but even more important than the *laws* of the Sabbath was *the Lord* of the Sabbath. He is also Lord of our homes, marriages, families, and other institutions that have rules as their framework. Rules and role descriptions are good, but *God does not ask us to appoint ourselves martyrs and prune everything in our personalities that does not fit into a role description.* That's *his* job. Throughout our lives he gradually prunes away the traits in us that are not Christlike so that our relationships can grow and bear good fruit. Just as man was not made for the Sabbath but the Sabbath for man, so relationships were not made to fit into precise formulas. Rather, biblical role descriptions were given as guidelines for the good of relationships.

Submitting Our Spiritual Best to God

*Of all the Spiritual Disciplines, none has been more abused
than the Discipline of submission.* —Richard Foster[3]

The strength to live with integrity in our relationships comes only from trusting in Christ instead of ourselves or in those we put on pedestals. Living with integrity frees us from idolizing relationship ideals. It frees us to find the safety of submitting to God, first and last. But it does not guarantee impressive results or even successful relationships. God gives each person the privilege of deciding whether or not he or she will put him first—in every situation.

The love and acceptance we experience in our relationship with Christ moves us to respond to others with love and acceptance because they are on the way, just as we are. Laying aside our critical demands and unrealistic expectations encourages others to acknowledge their own weaknesses and trust Christ to continue his good work in their lives.

During my first years of marriage to Frank, I, too, had looked at those role descriptions of wives and husbands under a microscope, skipping over the verses preceding them. I tried to be so careful to be subject to Frank's authority, to submit to him as my head, but I didn't know what that meant, and I kept getting hurt over and over.

Frank was the peaceful, easygoing, when-I-get-around-to-it type. Yet my way of reining myself in, waiting for my husband to fit into an idealized picture of biblical leadership, didn't appear to work. It was a strange dilemma. I wanted to fit in with Frank's plans, to respect him, to follow his leadership. Yet I didn't know what to do with some of the strengths God had given to me. I often waited for Frank to make decisions, to speak up for me, to protect me. Sometimes I ended up hurt, disappointed, and angry.

Several years after Frank and I were married, we moved to a small cottage in the country. We'd recently been devastated by news of the moral downfall of a dearly beloved pastor in our former church. Because our new home was miles away, we looked for a new church closer to our new home and began attending one with stricter rules than we were used to. I suppose at that time, the idea of a group of people who could keep rules appeared to hold out a guarantee of moral purity in the church—something we were hungry for (although I know keeping rules doesn't guarantee the development of strong, godly character). The new pastor knew the Bible more thoroughly than anyone we'd known before, and we respected his knowledge.

The pastor was in need of a secretary who could also help him counsel women and plan women's ministry activities. So when he asked me to take the job, Frank and I figured and refigured our budget until I could accept the position, even though it meant a significant cut in salary. I wasn't a professional counselor at the time, but the pastor said he'd noticed that women naturally came to talk to me and that I appeared to have the spiritual gifts of mercy and exhortation. I agreed to take the job and looked forward to the work.

After only a few weeks, Frank and I began to suspect that we might be out of place in that church. Women received a sound reminder each Sunday that they were to submit to their husbands at all costs, yet there was no mention of husbands' responsibility to love their wives. On weekdays, when women came to the church for counseling, the pastor saw them himself instead of referring any of them to me. This surprised me because earlier he had explained that he thought it was better for women to talk with a female counselor since many of their concerns were of a personal nature. I decided I should wait patiently until he began making referrals to me. After all, he was the pastor.

As fall approached, I started planning the women's retreat, consulting with him as I went along. As women began signing up to attend, I overheard the pastor and his wife ridiculing several of them for needing to spend time away from their husbands, indicating to me that they had no grasp of the soul's need for rest and restoration. They implied that it was a bad thing for women to want some time away for themselves. Before the date of the retreat arrived, several women decided not to go after all. One morning as I walked into the church kitchen to get a cup of coffee, the pastor and another man were laughing about how the man's wife had not completed all the chores he'd listed for her so he'd taken the car away from her for the day as punishment, which the two men found amusing. I soon realized that it was not only the pastor but also some of the men in leadership positions who seemed to think that women's needs weren't important.

At night I'd complain to Frank about that church's twisted perceptions of the role of women, especially related to submission to their husbands. I complained about my job and the pastor's legalistic views and suggested to Frank that we should find another church. Yet I was too afraid to bring up any of these concerns with the pastor. I expected Frank to share my viewpoints, somehow fix things, and keep me safe by making the decision to leave.

But Frank was having his own business problems. His work restoring custom cars, which had thrived for years, appeared to be headed for bankruptcy, and a lot of Frank's energy went to trying to keep things financially afloat. Although he listened to my complaints and requests, he was preoccupied with his problems at work.

For the first time, I felt lonely in my marriage to Frank and angry at the pastor as I tried to find some way to fit in with my friends at church. Some of the women started phoning me to talk about their feelings of oppression and discouragement. They blamed themselves because their husbands were not happy or pleased with them. None of us understood that we were responsible for our own emotional well-being. We also didn't realize that we'd lost integrity in our relationships and had become entangled in the malicious practice of gossip. These conversations with other women became a pseudoconsolation for the ministry work I'd hoped to take part in at this church, even though it felt as if I were sneaking crumbs from underneath someone else's dinner table.

One day a woman phoned the church to talk to the pastor, but he was busy, so she tearfully told me about her problem. Her husband had pushed her up against a wall, hit her, and threatened to hit their son. She was concerned and had called the church to talk it over with the pastor. As soon as he was free, I went into his office to recount the woman's story, assuming he would want to help. It never entered my mind that he wouldn't want to hear the story, but before I could get the details out, he interrupted: "You think too much."

I sat in my chair, stunned. His words stung like a slap in the face. For the first time, I saw clearly that this pastor didn't place much value on the emotional well-being of women. He wasn't especially concerned about their safety or protection—only that they submit to their husbands in all situations. I also saw that women in this church, including me, had learned to ignore their own instincts as they tried to follow precise directions about submitting to their husbands and the pastor, no matter what. The sad fact was that we were no longer submitting to God as our highest authority.

The next day I resigned, and Frank and I left the church. It would be some months before we could face entering a church again. All of our friends in that church, with the exception of two or three, refused to speak to us because the pastor had forbidden us to leave, saying it was the elders' decision whether we should leave—not ours. But it had become clear to us that God was not respected as sovereign in that church.

The situation had taken its toll on our emotions. Before we left, Frank tried to reason with the pastor and explain why we were leaving, but he got only a sound scolding in return. We had tried to do the right things, but we were overwhelmed. My spirit was deflated. I had become confused about the character of God. I felt as if my husband, my pastor, the church, and God had all let me down. It would take time before I realized that it wasn't God who had let me down. It was my idealized expectations of authorities—both my husband and my pastor—that had let me down.

Self-Martyrdom Doesn't Work

Later, as I looked back on this experience, I realized that my fear, self-doubt, and self-abandonment drove me to take on the self-appointed role of martyr. I had let my priorities get scrambled and paid a higher price for working in the ministry than God was asking of me. I had also ignored my own instincts about what was going on and lost track of my true knowledge of the Lord.

I had taken the job as an avenue of ministry, a way to offer my gifts. But over time, trust had broken down between the pastor and me and, later, between Frank and me. God had given me the privilege of thinking, forming opinions, having preferences, standing in my place as his woman, and having honest relationships. But I didn't know how to hold on to these privileges in a church that denied them.

I was deeply hurt. Evil had sprung up in the church—a place where I did not expect to find it. And now evil was springing up in my own heart as I angrily lashed out at my husband. I blamed him for not protecting me, not making the decision to leave the church, not speaking up on my behalf. In my well-intentioned but immature efforts to be a godly, submissive wife, I had lost track of the larger goal—the goal of submitting myself to God first.

I've shared this story not to rag on the church—the last thing it needs is more bad press. I am also not suggesting that people should leave a church just because they disagree with the pastor or others in the church or because the pastor may be strict. He may also be loving, humble, and just, a leader who is submitting his heart to God above all others. But if there is a threat to people's physical safety or if people's spirits are oppressed, discuss your concerns with your pastor. Frank tried this, and the pastor's response revealed that although he dogmatically preached women's submission to their husbands, he himself was not in submission to God's authority.

I don't bring up the issue of abuse within the church to stir up suspicion of pastors and church leaders. Of course we are to respect and honor them. But they are to be submissive to God above all others, even above their own need to feel in control. From my own experience and from talking with others, I believe that abuse of the biblical doctrine of submission within the church leaves women wounded and deeply confused because it occurs while they are trying hard to do the right thing, to serve in their churches, and to submit to God and other authority figures they thought would be trustworthy. These women are left wondering, *Was that abuse? Was it my fault? Is this what God is like?* The abuse devalues their femininity, causes them to doubt themselves and feel ashamed if they can't quickly forgive and get over the damage inflicted by abusive or unsafe authority figures in the church, where they expected to find safety and loving acceptance.

Ignoring our own safety instincts is often a sign that we're putting ourselves on the cross and trying to make sacrifices that only Jesus could make, trying to do what only Jesus could do. Self-imposed martyrdom never works because it makes us too big and God too small. It tries to force submission, which is impossible because true submission is offered freely. As God strengthens us internally, we become wiser, more discerning, and more committed to living with integrity. Our instincts for safety help us recognize untrustworthiness, and we need to pay attention to them.

In the following months and even years, Frank and I would both need God's healing so that we could return to church as a place of worship, study, and community life, a place where we could submit ourselves to God and learn to trust authorities in the church again. It would take time, restoration in the company of safe people, and a more fierce yieldedness to God above any other authorities.

Our quest would send us on a journey deeper into the heart of God, past precise relationship ideals we had once idolized and beyond our shortsighted, unrealistic expectations of others. What we are still discovering is this: *It takes far more of Christ's strength for us to keep him—not ourselves or someone else—on the throne of our hearts than it takes to follow an ideal model or role description.* True biblical submission asks that we become *more* honest, not hide our strengths or act as if we're not supposed to have them. It asks that we be *more* accountable for the abilities and gifts God has entrusted to us.

Ignoring our own safety instincts is often a sign that we're putting ourselves on the cross, trying to make sacrifices only Jesus could make and do what only Jesus could do.

It also creates a need to learn new skills so that we are able to ask questions and respectfully bring up topics we think need to be addressed even if it creates tension—and even with our leaders. This is yet another way in which Christ strengthens us as we submit to him before all others. Our lives may be less likely to impress others, but true biblical submission offers an opportunity to trust Christ together and acknowledge that *he* is in control—not any of us.

Are there ways in which you play the self-appointed martyr, expecting more of yourself than God does? Do you idolize *ideals* for relationships more than you revere God himself? You may be settling for role-playing when he wants his love to flow through you as you respectfully submit yourself to him before every-thing—and everyone—else.

Let Christ possess you. . . . Let him be the Lord of every
phase of your life. —Billy Graham[4]

● ● ● ● ● ● ● ● ● ● ● ● ● ● ●

REFLECT ON THE TRUTH

The following questions and exercises are intended to help you
prayerfully reflect on what you have read. You might want to use a
notebook or journal for writing down your thoughts, feelings, and
prayers as you go along.

Self-Imposed Martyrdom Is Not Biblical Submission

1. Open with prayer.

2. Read Psalm 1. Then go back and read verses 1-3 again.

3. Read Ephesians 5. What does it mean to be an imitator of God?
   How will imitating God affect your relationships in a marriage?
   in parenting? in your extended family? with your friends? in the
   workplace?

4. What one or two attributes of God's character will you ask him to
   build into you because it will help you to have stronger, health-
   ier relationships?

5. Have you ever played the self-appointed martyr? Reflect
   on ways you may do that now. How is this different from trusting in God?

6. Close in prayer, ending with the prayer of surrender: "Lord,
   thank you for loving and accepting me. I turn over to you my
   heart, mind, body, and soul. All that I am belongs to you,
   through Christ, who loved me and gave himself for me.
   Amen."

TAKE THE TRUTH WITH YOU

Living with integrity as I trust Christ and others does not guarantee "impressive" results. Therefore, I will respectfully submit myself to God as my highest authority. I will not expect more of myself than he does. I will not expect more of others than he does. That way, I will be free to enjoy his company and to serve him and others.

PART
TWO

Exchanging Myths
for the Truth

Jesus doesn't change—yesterday, today,
tomorrow, he's always totally himself.
Don't be lured away from him by the
latest speculations about him. The grace
of Christ is the only good ground for life.
Products named after Christ don't seem to
do much for those who buy them.

HEBREWS 13:8-9,
THE MESSAGE

5

The Truth Will Set You Free

Jesus said, "You shall know the truth and the truth shall make you free." Well, frankly, we know a lot of truth, but it's not making us free. —John Eldredge[1]

❦

THE MYTH: If my faith is strong enough, God will fix my problems.

> Because of the sacrifice of the Messiah, his blood poured out on the altar of the Cross, we're a free people—free of penalties and punishments chalked up by all our misdeeds. And not just barely free, either. *Abundantly* free! EPHESIANS 1:7, *THE MESSAGE*

In the eighth chapter of the Gospel of John, Jesus is explaining to the Jews the truth about his identity as the Son of God. He knew where he had come from, where he was headed, and that he and his heavenly Father were one. Living in the light of this truth made him free. Yet the more Jesus tried to explain who he was, the more indignant, defensive, and angry his Jewish listeners e, until finally they picked up rocks and began to throw them at him. *Even with Jesus right in front of them, the Jews could not believe he was the Son of God.* It was a transcendent spiritual reality—and they missed it!

As Christians, we may *want* to live as God desires and fulfill his purpose for us. We may *want* to live in truth and freedom as Jesus did because his heart belonged to God. But often we are like those Jewish listeners: We are bound by our dependence on physical realities and blind to spiritual realities. We mistake what we can verify with our physical senses for reality. When we face problems, we may tend to assume that we've done something wrong or have failed to exercise enough faith or pray hard enough. From there, it's only a small step to believing that if our faith is strong enough, God will change or fix the problems in our lives and that will make us free. Because of this misperception about the relationship between the level of our faith and our problems, we're afraid even to admit that we have problems because doing so would mean that our faith is weak.

Yet in the spiritual life, the opposite is true. Having strong faith means trusting God *beyond* what we can see, beyond what is obvious. Only as we find ourselves covered in God's grace, whether our circumstances are pleasant or painful, are we really free. Instead of denying that we have problems, we need to face them, trust Christ to make us stronger through them, and pray for the solutions we hope for.

Christ transcends any problems we may encounter. He will faithfully nurture and strengthen us in his grace, whether we get the results we want or not. If we cannot see the spiritual reality that lies beyond our painful circumstances—especially when God does not change those circumstances in response to our prayers—we may become bitter or spiteful toward others. We will not be living in freedom because we will be in bondage to our own misperceptions and misplaced desires.

How Many Fingers Do You See?

The film *Patch Adams* gives a vivid illustration of the value of seeing beyond the obvious. Near the beginning of the movie, Arthur Mendelson, one of the patients at a psychiatric hospital and a scientific genius, presents the newly admitted Hunter Adams with a riddle:

"How many fingers do you see?" Arthur asks, thrusting four fingers in front of Hunter's face.

"Four," Hunter replies.

"Idiot!" shouts Arthur impatiently, dismissing Hunter as just one more person who can't see what's right in front of his nose.

Later, Hunter pays a visit to Arthur's room and asks him to reveal the secret of the riddle. At first Arthur ignores Hunter, but after Hunter uses a strip of tape to stop a slow leak in Arthur's plastic cup, Arthur turns in his chair to face his new friend, whom he appropriately nicknames "Patch."

"How many fingers do you see?" Arthur asks with more patience, again holding up four.

"Four fingers, Arthur."

"No, no, no. Look at me," Arthur persists. "Look at me. You're focusing on the problem." Patch appears confused as Arthur goes on. "If you focus on the problem, you can't see the solution. Never focus on the problem. Look at me. How many do you see?" Arthur awaits Patch's reply with uncharacteristic, childlike anticipation. "Look *beyond* the fingers. How many do you see?"

Straining to catch the moment's meaning, Patch stares at Arthur's face with the four fingers in front of it. Suddenly his visual image of the four fingers begins to blur out of focus and into double images.

"Eight," whispers Patch.

"Yes! Yes! Yes!" exclaims Arthur, like a joyful parent watching a five-year-old pedal off on his bike without training wheels for the first time.

Patch's first answer to the riddle had been the obvious—the four fingers in plain view. But as Arthur coaxed Patch to look beyond the problem, he discovered something unexpected—a new way of seeing what was right in front of him by focusing intently on what was in the background.

As Christians, how do we get beyond our initial misperceptions so that we can stay close to Christ, live honestly and authentically as Jesus did, and biblically submit to God in the midst of our problems? If we're going to walk in truth and freedom, the first thing we need to do is admit that we have a problem.

Acknowledge Your Problems

When we're struggling with difficulties, it's tempting to ignore the pain, deny its damage, or stay busy so we don't have to think about it. But we need to be honest about what has actually happened to us in our churches, our families, and our close relationships. This often means accepting a reality we don't want to accept and acknowledging that something we don't want to be true is true: A beloved child has cancer. A young adult has chosen a prodigal journey and is now chemically addicted. A pastor may have been caught in an adulterous relationship and has left town. We don't want these things to be true, but they are.

In Mark 4, Jesus' disciples are in a boat when a great windstorm arises. Jesus is asleep in the stern. The fearful disciples, doubting Jesus' care for them, rush to wake him, and he stops the storm and calms the waves. At this point the disciples are in awe. But if they had denied that there was a problem—in this case, the violent storm—they would have missed the opportunity to see

Jesus' power in the midst of it. In the same way, if we don't acknowledge our own problems, we miss the opportunity to see the power of Christ that lies beyond them.

Is there a reality God is prompting you to accept, a wound in need of healing, a secret that needs to be exposed to the light of Christ? If so, don't try to go it alone. A heavy dose of reality can threaten to overwhelm you if you sit alone with it. Find a trustworthy friend to talk to, someone who can handle looking at life as it really is. Get together with someone in your church who has a mature faith and understands that God is the God of all reality, not only of what we can see in front of our noses. You may also decide to seek support from a Christian counselor, someone who can help you face difficult realities and then work with you as you take the next step: learning to look beyond the obvious.

Look beyond the Obvious

Remember the riddle of the four fingers? As Christians, we encounter a similar riddle in our spiritual lives when we face a problem. First we need to acknowledge what is right in front of us: our problem (similar to counting the fingers that someone is holding up in front of us). But that is only the beginning. As Patch Adams did, we need to learn to look *beyond* the obvious and gain a perspective about what is going on beyond our problems.

Is there a reality God is prompting you to accept, a wound in need of healing, a secret that needs to be exposed to the light of Christ?

All of us have wounds because we live in a fallen world. Jesus is our supreme example of someone wounded at the hands of others. If it happened to him, it will also happen to us, in our families, churches, and communities. But Jesus knew that behind his suffering and woundedness, there was a greater purpose: the redemption of his people.

When we are in emotional pain or experience disappointment or disillusionment, God may be prompting us to acknowledge a problem we have not yet faced. He may be stretching our faith, inviting us to grow stronger in our inner woman, and through his strength get out of the pattern of misperceptions we're entangled in. Embracing this challenge leads to more authentic, truthful living, becoming more alive in our relationship with him and increasingly dying to self.

We may know objectively that God is at work behind the scenes, but only as our gaze remains fixed on Christ, do our problems begin to blur out of focus. We need to find ways to acknowledge the cares of this world and yet see them, no matter how devastating, against the backdrop of Christ's redemptive sacrifice on the cross and what he wants to do in us through our problems.

See Jesus as the Solution

> Jesus said to the people who believed in him, "You are
> truly my disciples if you keep obeying my teachings.
> And you will know the truth, and the truth will set
> you free." JOHN 8:31-32, NLT

We've talked about the importance of honestly acknowledging the reality of our problems and of learning to look beyond them. But unless we look to Jesus as the solution and the source of healing and restoration, we will be unable to die to ourselves and our own desires and truly submit ourselves to his will for us.

It's inherent in human nature to not want to have—let alone solve—problems and to resist change. Life is not ideal for most of us, and it can be painful to look realistically at our problems, whether they result from wrongs done to us, wrongs we've done to others, or just circumstances that have turned out differently from what we had hoped. Yet it is here and only here—in the midst of suffering that cuts deep into our souls—that we find out how big God is. There is only one cure for our problems: God's restorative, healing grace. His truth, love, and beauty transcend any hypocrisy, hatred, or ugliness we can name.

I was leading a retreat on the West Coast. The earlier sessions had gone well, and the women were looking forward to some leisure time on Saturday afternoon. Several of them planned to hike one of the trails through the coastal redwoods or relax on the beach. Others were going to attend a discussion group I was to lead.

When I arrived for the group meeting, we decided to arrange the chairs in a semicircle in front of the window so that we could gaze at the giant redwoods as we talked to each other. The women shared cautiously at first and then gradually began to open up and become more vulnerable. Soon they were exchanging opinions about everything from PMS, to problems in their relationships with their mothers, to the best ways to teach stress management to your children when you're stressed to the max yourself.

Near the end of our time together, one woman spoke up matter-of-factly, saying she'd been sexually molested when she was nine years old and had never told anyone. As she talked, I was struck by her apparent lack of feeling about such a painful memory. I hung around later as the other women were leaving to see if she wanted to talk further. But since she was talking quietly with a friend and seemed to be on the verge of tears, I decided to leave them alone and try to check with her later.

A Communion service was planned for the next morning after the general session. Now, I realize that not everyone reading this book is comfortable with the idea of observing the Lord's Supper outside of a church service in which there are ordained leaders present, but the retreat had been planned to include this element of worship. The narrator read a passage from Mark 14, and five women took their places at the front of the sanctuary to serve Communion.

I was sitting in one of the front rows, so I was among the first to be served. As I returned to my place after receiving Communion and waited for others to be served, I tried to absorb the beauty of the moment as women filed by the servers to partake of the bread and the cup, music played, and voices softly whispered, "The body of Christ; take, eat. The blood of Christ, poured out for you."

Suddenly there was a piercing scream from the back of the room. Some people turned around to see what was happening, and I noticed it was the woman who told the small group she'd been abused as a child. She cried out again and again before breaking into sobs and falling to the floor. The leader looked anxiously at the woman and then at me, as if wondering what she should do.

My personal anxiety and professional instincts urged me to shout, "Stop! You're having a flashback, and this should happen only in a counselor's office with careful pacing!" But my heart instincts overruled my anxiety, and I walked over and knelt beside the woman on the floor, along with three or four who had already come to quietly pray. The woman's deep cries and groans arose from the back of the sanctuary, accompanied by soft whispers of prayer from the lips of sisters in the Lord who were surrounding her as the voices of the servers and the music mingled in the background. Outcry, loving support, God's comfort, the serving of the elements—all of these were happening at once. Somehow I knew that the moment's meaning was beyond what I could take in or describe.

Soon the sobbing quieted, the woman lifted her head, wiped away her tears, and slowly rose to her feet. Flanked on either side by the steadying arms of friends, she made her way to the front of the sanctuary. After the woman had received the elements of Communion, she turned to walk back to the pew where she'd been sitting. As she did, five or six tearful women stood and began applauding softly. Then others stood, and others, and soon every woman in the room was on her feet, clapping softly, until the woman reached the back of the sanctuary and collapsed into her seat wearing a weary but peaceful smile.

Nobody could put into words what happened that day because it's almost always impossible to capture the essence of a spiritual experience in words. But we all knew it had something to do with the truth of Christ's sacrificial death overshadowing all of our human pain and suffering, accompanied by God's compassionate comfort through whispers of prayer and music. That woman had faced up to a very painful reality in the supportive company of Christ's people and had found Christ as the solution. We had partaken of his sacramental love, wrapped in a unifying moment of transcendent grace.

The God of reality is not bound by time. He is able to enter into your life at any moment of your history and wrap you in his grace, no matter what the problem in your life has been. We can trust him to be the solution beyond what we can see at the moment. Ironically, even when we have carefully set up a support system to help us as we work at acknowledging our problems and looking beyond them, God in his sovereignty sometimes chooses to bypass our well-laid plans for finding healing and instead reveals himself as the solution in an unexpected way. He chose to do that for that woman—and the rest of us that day—in a way none of us could have expected or will ever forget.

Living Free

> [Jesus said,] "You are the light of the world. A city on
> a hill cannot be hidden. Neither do people light a
> lamp and put it under a bowl. Instead they put it on
> its stand, *and it gives light to everyone in the house.*"
> MATTHEW 5:14-15 (emphasis added)

When we can admit the truth about our lives as fully as God has revealed it to us in any moment, problems and all, and see it against the backdrop of Christ's sacrificial love for us, we don't have to play games, defend ourselves, or hide our true selves from others. We don't have to try to detect all the evils of our hearts and expose them all at once. Jesus takes care of that, gently revealing the truth to us by his Spirit as we are ready, one day at a time. All we need to do is ask: "Search me, O God, and know my heart; test me and know my anxious thoughts. See if there is any offensive way in me, and lead me in the way everlasting" (Psalm 139:23-24).

If we are willing to go through the dark moments of life holding hands with Jesus, he will illumine our way and lead us as we live in truth we have not yet discovered. Christ has offered us a better way to live by looking beyond what we can touch, feel, or predict with our senses. It's a little like Arthur said to Patch Adams: "See what others choose *not* to see, out of fear, conformity, and laziness. See the whole world anew each day." As we trust Christ in the midst of even the darkest reality, he will empower us to live more and more in his strength and less and less in the bondage of realities we refuse to accept. This is a significant step in learning to die to self, to become alive to God, and to live the life he has called us to live.

On a trip to Flathead Valley, Montana, set against the dramatic backdrop of Glacier National Park, Frank and I flew to Kalispell and then drove to the campground where we were to stay. I was amused by some of the place-names: Hungry Horse. Whitefish. Big Arm. Burnt Fork. Even walking paths had names, like Bear Dance Trail, and the ski slope in the park was called The Big Mountain. As is typical of many Indian names, the names described what was true of those places or what had happened there.

I began to wish for a similar way for Christians to strip down our names to what describes what is really true of the lives we live. It would simplify things, cut through the smoke screens we put up for ourselves and each other, and clarify whether or not we're living up to the names God calls us to live by. I wondered, if our names reflected our *lived life*—the way Indian names described each individual—what would our names be?

Many people, even Christians, live a lot of years with false names—their *lived lives* do not reflect what God has called them to live according to his purpose for them. I lived a lot of years by the name Princess Hides Herself. From around the age of twelve until I was forty-something, that name described how I lived because I thought that was what it meant to die to self and let Christ live inside me. The freedom of spirit that Jesus talked about eluded me, although I wouldn't admit it.

I grew up with the misperception that I was not supposed to be strong. It seemed to me that only one girl in the family could be strong, and that was my older sister's job. *I* was supposed to be good. No one at home talked about this or told me directly; I just perceived that's what I was supposed to do: be a good girl. As a child or young person, when someone wounded me or violated my rights, I assumed it would not have happened if I had been good enough. *Being good enough* became the measuring stick for my sense of value and significance, and since I never quite made it, I didn't know what it was to be free in spirit.

Did you have a similar perception about yourself when you were growing up? Was your perceived measuring stick academic performance? athletic performance? the ability to get along with others? being nice? Perhaps you thought you were supposed to be the perfect one, the strong one, the weak one, the one who always took care of Mom or Dad, or the one who always got into trouble. Are you still living by this false standard instead of in the value and freedom you have through Christ's sacrificial death?

I carried my ingrained false measurement of value with me into my first marriage, the church, jobs, and even to some extent into my second marriage. Gradually, I began to discover that I was not living the life God had called me to live, in truth, freedom, and light, partly because of *my misperceptions* of what my family and others expected of me. I yearned to experience real freedom in Christ and to claim and live by my real name, but I didn't know how. I didn't even know what my real name was.

My sister, Jan, on the other hand, has always known her real name. She has always loved life, people, animals, plants, and good food. As far back as I can remember, she has known the deepest truths of her soul—what she liked and loved, what she lived for and would die for. Her real name would be Princess Happy Sunflower. Jan's wonderful smile, hearty laugh, and generous hospitality attract many friends.

As I began my search for the name God called me to live by, I had to face problems and accept realities I did not like. Doing so was often painful, and I avoided it for as long as I could. I had to learn how to forgive people who had wronged me. I had to learn to accept responsibility for pain I had caused others, to ask for God's forgiveness, and to forgive myself when God shined the light of his truth into my heart and exposed my pride, idolatry, jealousy, and other sins.

This is not easy. It has always been difficult for people to live truthfully, in freedom, and not hide themselves. Adam and Eve hid from God after they sinned in the Garden of Eden. But God only wanted them to admit the truth, return to his side, and walk closely with him. He wanted them to live by a divine reality that transcends all of the realities of this world—the reality of their identity as children of God.

If you are going to replace the myth that you've been living with the truth, the first step is to admit that you have not been true to yourself—that is, to what God has called you to be—and thus, you have not been true to God. As I looked at my realities against the backdrop of the sacrificial death of Christ and focused day by day on the knowledge that his infinite grace goes far beyond my sins, I gained a new vision for the life God had called me to live. I began to love character strengths I did not yet possess but longed for—like courage and integrity. I started to see ways God was using my problems to stretch me and help me grow in grace and learn to love in a more biblically mature way.

With God's help, I started living with more freedom and trans-parency. The name Princess Hides Herself no longer fit because it did not allow the light of Christ to shine through me. It did not reflect the growing freedom of my spirit in Christ.

I decided to choose a new name to live by, one that reflects the life I believe God calls me to live and the person God knows I truly am but I am only gradually discovering. My new name is Princess Walks-in-the-Light. I want more than anything to live in God's light and truth, to let his searchlight keep exposing more of the dark places in my heart so that he can fill me more and more with his light. I know I won't ever live up to my name perfectly, but that's not the point. It is a name that gives me hope because it reveals my heart's deepest desire.

Sometimes people ask why I am so vulnerable in my writing and speaking and share so many of my weaknesses and imperfec-

I do it because it is the only way I know to show God's light love—by letting them shine brightly through the cracks in my broken life. He reigns over everything I cannot control, but I can worship and walk beside him because of his transcendent grace. More than anything, I want to walk in the light—not hide myself. I want my life to reveal God's glory.

What's Your Name?

When we think about the people who have given us hope and have increased the strength of our soul, we might discover that they were not the advice givers, warners or moralists, but the few who were able to articulate in words and actions the human condition in which we participate, and who encouraged us to face the realities of life. —Henri Nouwen[2]

Are you living by a name that reflects the deepest desire God has rooted in your heart—the life God calls you to live for his glory? Or are you living by a name that holds you in bondage to realities you won't accept? If so, it's time to open your eyes to what is in front of your face. Ask God to give you grace to trust him with all your heart. Then admit what is true about your life—what happened, sins committed against you, and sins you have committed against others—without being defensive. Then look beyond it all, and focus on Christ and his death on the cross, the power of his grace that transcends the power of sin. Hold your focus there, on Christ. Draw it back again and again until the problems in the foreground blur out of focus and you are able to see Christ as your solution.

Jesus, who knows it all and is with us through it all, calls us to a life of freedom and truth. He is the reality that transcends all of our problems, sins, wounds—anything we can name about ourselves. He is ultimate reality, and he calls us to live by our real names.

82

I am Princess Walks-in-the-Light. What is your name?

> You are the ones chosen by God, chosen for the high
> calling of priestly work, chosen to be a holy people,
> God's instruments to do his work and speak out for
> him, to tell others of the night-and-day difference he
> made for you—from nothing to something, from
> rejected to accepted.   1 PETER 2:9-10, *THE MESSAGE*

● ● ● ● ● ● ● ● ● ● ● ● ● ● ●

REFLECT ON THE TRUTH

The following questions and exercises are intended to help you
prayerfully reflect on what you have read. You might want to use a
notebook or journal for recording your thoughts, feelings, and
prayers.

The Truth Will Set You Free

1. Open with prayer.

2. Read Psalm 31:1-5. The first step in transcending a problem is
   accepting the reality that there is a problem. This sounds so
   simple, but we tend to deny, idealize, or avoid talking about our
   problems. God wants us to turn to him daily—problems, confusion, and all. He already knows that our faith is small, and he
   loves us anyway.

3. Can you think of a time when you acknowledged a reality you did not want to face and discovered Christ's power beyond it? What were the circumstances? Write your thoughts in your journal.

4. When you were growing up, was there a myth you perceived you were supposed to live up to? What did you think was expected of you: to be the strong one? the smart one? the bad one? the good one? the incapable one? something else? How did you respond? What effect did it have on your later life (e.g., in marriage or with your children or in your life with God)? Often you can identify the myth or misperception by thinking about what you tend to overdo on: taking care of others, being overresponsible, overworking, etc.

5. As God's children, we are called to walk in truth and light. We are intended to live by the names of our true selves. What is the name of your true self—the person God knows you are? Use a princess name, because as God's child, you are a daughter of the King. Your true name will be connected to your gifts and to the deepest desires of your heart. Identifying them will help you choose a name that really fits you as God intends you to live.

   [Jesus said,] "You are the light of the world. A city on a hill cannot be hidden. Neither do people light a lamp and put it under a bowl. Instead they put it on its stand, and it gives light to everyone in the house. In the same way, let your light shine before men, that they may see your good deeds and praise your Father in heaven."   Matthew 5:14-16

6. Close in prayer, ending with the prayer of surrender. "Father, thank you for loving and accepting me. I turn over to you my heart, mind, body, and soul. All that I am belongs to you, through Christ, who loved me and gave himself for me. Amen."

TAKE THE TRUTH WITH YOU

Instead of denying my problems, I will accept the truth about myself as God reveals it to me. I will learn to face those problems, pray for the solutions I hope for, and trust Christ to make me stronger through them because he is always beyond them.

6

Truth and Consequences

[Jesus] learned the pain of rejection and the sorrow of unre-
quited love. We learn to feel in much the same way. When
our faith is tested in some wilderness. When our best-laid
plans go awry and our bravest prayers go unanswered.

—Ken Gire[1]

**THE MYTH: If I honestly admit my feelings, they will
control me.**

"What are you doing with your anger?" the counselor asked, lean-
ing so far forward I thought he might tip out of his chair.

"Anger?" I sniffed, my eyes brimming with tears. "I'm not
angry."

I had been insisting that I had forgiven my first husband for
leaving me after fifteen years of marriage and that I was fine, fine,
fine. No anger here.

I was a Christian, and I thought good Christians didn't get
mad—or if they did, they didn't "let the sun go down" on it. They
were supposed to forgive quickly, because that's what it says to do
in the Bible. So I tried really hard to not think angry thoughts or
act in anger, mistakenly reasoning that this meant I was not angry.

All of this was part of my attempt to die to self, as I thought the Bible described. I had even shown my counselor written proof of my righteousness: prayer journals filled with poems of sadness and love—but no anger or fear.

Imagine my shock when the counselor responded, "I think you *are* mad, Brenda. *Really* mad." Shaken from my ivory tower of self-righteousness, I left his office sobbing and vowing I'd never go back. But he had loosened some of the stones in my wall of emotional resistance. The feelings of anger I had been denying were holding me captive, and I didn't even know it. My well-intentioned, though immature, reasoning was that if I admitted my real feelings, they would control me.

Being honest about my emotions was scary, but I had paid good money for that eyeball-to-eyeball confrontation, and I decided to pay some attention to the counselor's opinion.

Am I angry? I asked myself, trying to be honest. You *bet* I was angry. My marriage had been going downhill for some time, in spite of my best efforts to improve things, and now my husband had left home. Anger had been sitting on the back burner of my emotions until it had grown stale and cold and had turned into resentment. Was I fearful? I was worried sick. How would I feed my two boys and pay the bills? Was I hurt? I was hurt to the core. Not only had I lost my husband and my home; my reputation as a Christian woman was on the line, which unleashed more fear.

What a relief it was to finally begin to face these honest, though mixed-up, feelings in the presence of someone who cared enough to call my bluff and of a God who judged me far less harshly than I judged myself. I began to realize that God had created me with a full spectrum of feelings, like the colors in a rainbow. He didn't want me to ignore or deny the ones I'd rather not have any more than he wanted to erase a certain color in his rainbow just because it was not one of my favorites. God wanted me to recognize all my

feelings. Some of them, such as anger and fear, were sign̄
was time to look to him for direction, to think and act respon̄ı̄-
bly.

I was in my early thirties at the time. There have been other
times since then when I have again fallen into the trap of denying
my "undesirable" feelings while I tried to live as a submissive
Christian woman. This may have happened to you, too, though
perhaps under different circumstances. Who wants to have feelings like anger, fear, and disillusionment?

Yet when we disown our feelings, we actually disown part of
ourselves as God created us. *When we deny feelings we don't want to
have, we give them power to stunt our growth and short-circuit repentance.* We're trying to make the healing process work backward,
stuffing our emotions and acting strong (read, "trusting in
ourselves") instead of pouring out our feelings to God and trusting
him to strengthen us in our inner woman.

"Blessed are the pure in heart, for they will see God," Jesus said
in the Sermon on the Mount (Matthew 5:8). For the first time I
began to yearn for this purity of heart Jesus talked about, which
was so different from the self-deception going on in my heart as I
lied to myself about what I felt and tried to hide my emotions
from God. Purity of heart is related to honesty and trust. It's about
becoming strong internally, not merely pushing away my honest
feelings and *appearing strong.*

Fatal Attraction

Disowning feelings we don't want to have can have a subtle attrac-
tion, at least for a while. But when we ignore or suppress our feelings, their intensity builds. It is not possible to be submissive in a
healthy way if our emotions are just under the surface, waiting to
explode. Covering up hurts and disappointments in the name of
dying to self may cause us to deny or be blind to the need to

repent of sins that result from our cover-ups. If we feel put upon by others yet don't deal with our feelings honestly, we may "crawl onto the cross" and take on the role of martyr. If we bury our anger, it doesn't die—it smolders, intensifies, and turns into resentment. Then we become short-tempered, defensive, and critical, and our hearts become dull to our need to repent.

After my divorce, I finally had to start admitting how angry I was, how lonely I felt, how isolated I'd become. Facing these feelings began to dispel their power to subtly control my behavior and was the first step toward repentance and lasting change.

> *What am I doing*
> *in this lonesome chamber,*
> *looking so strong,*
> *feeling so weak?*
> *Why did I come?*
>
> *What consolation*
> *did I hope to find*
> *in this empty room*
> *with unspoken needs;*
> *my self betrayed?*
>
> *Why did I come*
> *to this desolate place*
> *and give up truth*
> *to gain these walls*
> *that close me in?*
>
> *What price do I pay*
> *to look so strong,*
> *to hide from God?*

I cannot pay. . . .
I am empty.
—Brenda Waggoner

Even though I didn't like feeling so empty, angry, afraid, and lonely, it was a relief to admit those feelings. Honesty opened my heart to God, and then he began to draw close to me and minister to my pain with his healing presence.

As we pour out our true feelings—fear, anger, frustration—to God, his Spirit teaches us how to handle them wisely, how to be angry and yet not sin, for example. When we admit our fear and let it drive us to God, he encourages us, empowers us, and holds us up, even if our knees continue to knock together. We can do difficult, scary things, even before we feel courageous, when we trust Christ instead of ourselves. Although we cannot voluntarily change our feelings, we *can* choose how we act and think. In time, God will change our feelings and emotions as we are honest about them and trust him. Exposed to God's redemptive grace, even hatred, bitterness, and resentment are transformed into love, joy, and gratitude.

Admitting our feelings helps ensure that they don't rule us. When the apostle Peter denied Christ, he felt healthy guilt and remorse, and those feelings of godly sorrow drove him to repentance. On the other hand, when Judas betrayed Christ, his feelings, whatever they were, did not result in repentance, and he took his life. Denied feelings build walls between ourselves and God and between ourselves and others and leave us isolated. Each time we deny our true feelings, we lay another brick in a wall of emotional dishonesty and deception. But eventually that wall will come crashing down.

Learning to Listen to Our Feelings
Recognizing our true feelings and listening to their messages is a vital part of growing strong in our inner woman. Disowning our

feelings is like staring past unwanted guests when they come knocking at our front doors, looking for the visitors we hoped would come instead. But those "unwanted guests" are going to come in anyway, so it's better to openly acknowledge their presence: *Hello, anger, fear, lust, jealousy. I see you're back. What message do you have for me today?* Otherwise, our front doors stand gaping as we look past these visitors (who are sure to come now and then) while they sneak in and hide, waiting to ambush us when we least expect it.

Only when we admit our weakness without Christ does he empower us with his strength. The Lord told Paul, "My power is made perfect in weakness" (2 Corinthians 12:9). Living with our feelings is part of living truthfully as Christians instead of clinging to "Christianized" mythical views of ourselves as people who never have feelings we don't want to have. The sooner we stop deceiving ourselves about our true feelings, the sooner we begin to grow through them and beyond them. Part of the grief process when we face losses is admitting *all* of our feelings, grieving what is true—what we must accept—and then, if others have wronged us, forgiving them. We must also forgive ourselves for falling short of all we hoped to be. When we surrender our pride and admit how much we need Christ, he cultivates purity in our hearts, reaffirms us as his blessed children, and gives us increased intimacy with him.

> [Jesus said,] "Whoever humbles himself like this child
> is the greatest in the kingdom of heaven."
>
> MATTHEW 18:4

When we are young children, being honest about our feelings comes easily. If we are sad or hurt, we run for comfort. When we're guilty, it shows on our faces, and after our parents discipline us, we usually feel better. Our relationship is restored and joy returns. Can you recall from your childhood how easy it was to recognize what you felt, to ask for what you needed or wanted, or to take responsibility for something you did wrong?

When I was a little girl, my family lived in the San Joaquin valley of California. Early one morning, instead of getting my usual wake-up call from my dad, I was awakened by the shaking of my bed from an earthquake. When I saw my porcelain Martha Washington doll had fallen off the shelf and broken into pieces, I dissolved into tears. I remember carefully picking up the large pieces that remained intact—head, feet, and body. But the neck and shoulders lay in a little pile of slivers on the linoleum floor.

After my dad checked the damage to the house, I showed him what was left of my doll. The expression on his face told me that Martha could not be put back together again. I felt sad and afraid because I didn't know what all the damage meant. I remember how my dad held me on his lap and how my fear and sadness turned into calmness as I lay my head on his chest. The need for comfort had driven me to my dad's arms, and although my immediate circumstances didn't change (my doll was gone for good), after spending a few minutes with my dad, I felt much better.

A couple of years later, some classmates and I were looking forward to going to see *The Old Man and the Sea,* which had just come out on the big screen. As I waited for my friends to arrive, I noticed my dad's change lying on top of his dresser. Although I was barely tall enough to see, I could tell that there was a big pile of pennies and a few nickels and dimes, enough to get a roll of NECCO wafers, a Baby Ruth, or a PayDay (a nickel apiece in those days). I usually got only one treat, but this was a special event, and as I stared at the mound of coins, I thought how fun it would be to get two things this time. After checking to make sure my dad was still outside, I dumped the contents of my little crocheted purse onto the bed and counted my pennies—there were eight.

Although I was not in the habit of stealing, I decided to take a couple of pennies from his pile so I'd have ten altogether. There were so many that I didn't think he'd notice that two were gone. I was sitting on the living-room couch, waiting for my friend's mom to pick me up, when my dad came into the room.

"Sue," he said, using his pet name for me, "let me see what's in your purse." I'm not sure whether a guilty look on my young face tipped him off, but I must have gulped hard as I loosened the drawstring to my purse and dumped out its contents for a second time. Instead of counting the pennies, Daddy picked up one of the coins I'd stolen, which was slightly bent on one side. I hadn't noticed that.

"Where did you get this penny?" he asked. Caught red-handed, I admitted what I had done and spent the afternoon scrubbing mold off our lawn chairs instead of watching *The Old Man and the Sea* and eating candy bars with my friends. I remember the healthy guilt that swept over me as my dad confronted me with my sin and how those feelings prompted me to be honest about what I had done (not that I could have weaseled my way out of it anyway). It felt good to quickly take responsibility for my actions instead of trying to live with the knowledge of it, though it wasn't the choice I would have made for myself as a seven-year-old.

As adults, we don't have our parents around to catch us in the act when we sin, so we need to practice catching ourselves and quickly confessing it to our heavenly Father. If our feelings remain tender toward Christ and the Holy Spirit's prompting, they help us by confronting us and motivating us to stay on track when we don't push them away. Like little red flags, they alert us that it's time to pay attention, to think and act responsibly. God never condemned his people for having feelings that are part of being human. In fact, the Scriptures are replete with his assurances to them when they were fearful, anxious, or weary. What got his people into trouble was their turning away from him and the actions that their unchecked feelings led to.

Acknowledged feelings lead to right actions and clear consciences; sometimes they act as catalysts for correcting a wrong course of action. Denied or unacknowledged feelings, on the other hand, lead to blaming others, blaming ourselves, and delayed growth. This is true today, and it's been true throughout history—even in Greek mythology.

Fleeing the Furies

The myth of Orestes contains a grain of truth about the importance of taking responsibility rather than denying the truth and about the role feelings play in the restoration process. The gods had placed a curse on the House of Atreus. Clytemnestra, Orestes' mother, had murdered both her husband and her father. This extended the curse down to Orestes, who, according to the Greek code of honor, was obligated to slay his father's murderer, in this case, his mother. To complicate things, in ancient Greece the greatest sin a person could commit was to kill his or her mother. After agonizing over his predicament, Orestes finally did what the code of honor required and killed Clytemnestra.

As punishment, the gods sentenced him to be pursued by the Furies—frightening, hissing, critical spirits whom only Orestes could see and hear. Orestes lived alone in his own private hell, chased by the Furies and wandering about, seeking a way to atone for his sin. After many years of this torture, he asked the gods to remove the curse and the Furies. At the trial, Apollo spoke in Orestes' defense, declaring that Clytemnestra's murder had actually been *his* fault since he had engineered the crime. He said that Orestes should not be held responsible since he had been left without a choice.

When Orestes heard this, he quickly arose and contradicted

Apollo: "It was I, not Apollo, who murdered my mother!" This amazed the gods, who had never before seen a member of the House of Atreus assume responsibility for his actions instead of blaming the gods. Not only did they remove the curse but they also transformed the Furies into the Eumenides—"bearers of grace"—loving spirits who would provide Orestes with wise counsel leading to good fortune thereafter.[3]

The transformation from torment to good fortune occurred because Orestes refused to allow someone else to take the blame for what he had done. He was honest about his actions and accepted full responsibility for them. Even though this is only a myth, its theme rings true for us: Often it is torment that drives us into the arms of our gracious Lord, where we learn to be honest and accept responsibility for our actions. Likewise, living in denial suspends us in a state of unawareness as we continue to do wrong, sin against God and others, and grow hardened in our hearts as we violate God's ways.

Admitting our feelings does *not* mean they will take control of us. Just the opposite is true. As we listen to what our feelings are saying, God makes us strong enough to obey his will in spite of them, even when they are quite intense and try to pull us in the opposite direction.

> *Blessedness is declared to be upon those who are not only poor and meek, but also mourners. This rules out any state of numbed emotional apathy.*
>
> —Simon Tugwell, theologian and author[4]

It may seem as if I'm really hammering away on the importance of facing up to our true feelings. But I believe avoiding our feelings is one of Satan's most powerful and deceptive weapons to keep Christians stuck in weakness and defeat. We cannot afford to "numb out," because being emotionally numb distracts us and keeps us off guard in much the same way people who have had too much to drink or are high on drugs aren't aware of what's going on around them. We no doubt recognize that using alcohol or other drugs to numb our emotions is wrong. But we're less likely to recognize the danger of numbing our alertness by denying our true feelings.

The Christlike approach is to pay attention to our feelings, grieve our losses, and accept the fact that there will always be some grief mixed in with life until we reach heaven. Instead, we often act as if sadness and grief are shameful and we should be able to bypass these undesirable feelings because we have Christ. We need to reconsider this mistaken understanding of feelings. Isaiah 53:3 says that Jesus was "a man of sorrows, and familiar with suffering." Grief dotted his earthly life from beginning to end. Listen to what G. K. Chesterton says about Christ and feelings:

> His pathos was natural, almost casual. The Stoics, ancient and modern, were proud of concealing their tears. He never concealed His tears; He showed them plainly on His open face at any daily sight, such as the far sight of His native city. . . . Solemn supermen and imperial diplomatists are proud of restraining their anger. He never restrained His anger. He flung furniture down the front steps of the Temple, and asked men how they expected to escape the damnation of Hell.[5]

Christ did hide some parts of himself from us, but not his feelings. In our desire to be like Jesus and to die to self, often the feelings we deny or work so hard not to feel are the very things God wants to use to strengthen and mature us, by asking us to admit the truth and to trust him in the midst if it.

Making Friends with Your Feelings

"I should be excited about my husband's commissioning as a missionary," said Barbara (not her real name). "I also sense the call to the work, and I don't exactly understand why, but I keep remembering what happened when my dad became a missionary."

Barbara's father had worked most of his life as a band director and lay pastor, dreaming of one day serving on a mission team overseas. During Barbara's high school years, her dad's dream had come true, and he and Barbara's mom went to Africa as missionaries, a real delight for them.

But it was a different story for Barbara. She lived with neighbors during part of her last two years of high school, and her parents missed all of her "senior moments": homecoming, prom, and even high school graduation. The idea of life in the ministry did not have particularly happy connotations for Barbara, although she also felt called to the work. "Every time Jim [her husband] talks about it, he gets so excited. I've tried to be excited with him, but for some reason my stomach ties up into knots, and sometimes I just go away by myself and wait it out."

Barbara's fears were natural in light of her previous experience related to mission work. She feared it might tear her family apart and separate her from her children, either geographically or emotionally. In time she began to see her anxiety as a helpful red flag that indicated the need for a firm commitment to honest communication among the family members as they served on the mission field. She and Jim decided to have family meetings once a week to discuss how things were going for everyone and to have quality time together. Aware of how easy it is for missionaries to put the priorities of their own families on the back burner, Barbara and Jim committed themselves to involvement in their children's activities and personal interests. Barbara's fear, once she admitted it and laid it in God's lap, led to the strengthening of their entire family.

How do you handle it when unwanted fear, worry, or anger plagues you? When you "make friends" with these undesirable feelings instead of run from them, you tap into a source of strength you don't have when you deny them. Have you heard the expression "You have to get right back on the horse"? It means that when a horse throws you, the best thing to do is get up and climb back on. Of course, *you're afraid to*. But when you confront what you fear or what makes you angry or jealous or lustful, you become stronger because it takes *Christ's* strength to face up to it. Gradually, Jesus turns our weaknesses into strengths for his glory, and when we look back, we see that it all started when we honestly faced our feelings.

Exchanging Resentment for Gratitude

The 1995 film *Dead Man Walking* illustrates how honesty and the willingness to accept responsibility for one's actions can open a person's heart to God's grace and turn once-denied offenses and unwanted regrets into sorrow, repentance, and gratitude. Death-row inmate Matthew Poncelet continues to deny the murder and rape he committed right up to the day of his execution. Sister Helen Prejean, who serves as his spiritual advisor, confronts him with the need to admit the truth and take responsibility for his actions.

> *When you confront what you fear or what makes you angry or jealous or lustful, you become stronger because it takes Christ's strength to face up to it.*

"Me and God, we got things all squared away," Matthew says. "I know Jesus died on the cross for us. I know he's gonna be there to take care of me on Judgment Day."

"Matt, redemption isn't some kind of free-admission ticket you get because Jesus paid the price. You gotta participate in your own redemption," says Sister Helen.

Sister Helen was off base when she told Matthew that we play a part in our own redemption. There is no part at all for us to play because Christ has done it all for us. The only thing we can do is admit the truth about our guilt and our need for Jesus. But when she suggests that Matthew read the Gospel of John, where Jesus said, "You will know the truth, and the truth will set you free" (John 8:32), Poncelet likes that. He wants to be free. But his only concept of freedom is getting out of prison. He keeps trying to figure out how Sister Helen can help him avoid death row by setting up an appeal, arranging for a lie detector test—anything. Just before Matthew's execution, Sister Helen presses him to talk about what happened the night of the crime. All along, he had stuck to his story that he only watched his friend rape a young woman in the woods and then kill her and the man who was with her.

"You could have just walked way," she challenges him. But Matthew keeps lashing out in anger, defending himself as a bystander and blaming his buddy, drugs, the government, even the two young people for being in the woods that night.

"What about Matthew Poncelet?" Sister Helen says. "Where is *he* in the story?"

Just minutes before Matthew is to make his walk to the death chamber, his real feelings finally spill over the thick wall of resentment, blame, and hatred he has built. He confesses to the crime. Tears of remorse stream down his cheeks as he lets the truth scour his crusty heart.

That is what happens to the human soul when we face the truth in the presence of God's redemptive love, when we confess deeds we've covered up and allow long-denied feelings to rise to the surface. Sister Helen helped Matthew Poncelet do that.

When we bury our feelings, we are all dead men and women walking. We blame others for what we have done, spew resentment, and wall ourselves off from others by living in denial. Only when we see the Matthew Poncelets in ourselves—guilty ones who must finally let down our emotional barriers—are we able to be filled with Christ, the redeemer of human sin, and be spiritual advisors to anyone else. Honest feelings and responsibility go hand in hand, leading us from resentment toward others to gratitude as the Holy Spirit envelops us in God's infinite grace.

When feelings come knocking at your door, look them straight in the eye. Listen to their messages. Don't let them sneak past you unaware to hide and jump out at you when you least expect them. Pay attention to them as signals to think and act responsibly. Then close the door, go into the presence of the Lord, who sits at the hearth of your soul, and have a fireside chat. If you feel fearful, angry, weary, jealous, admit your feelings quickly. Jesus will soothe and comfort you. If your feelings have built up over time, it may take many trips to the lap of God, but what's wrong with that?

There is no better place to be.

> Humble yourselves, therefore, under God's mighty
> hand, that he may lift you up in due time. Cast all
> your anxiety on him because he cares for you.
>
> 1 PETER 5:6-7

REFLECT ON THE TRUTH

The following questions and exercises are intended to help you prayerfully reflect on what you have read. You might want to use a notebook or journal for writing down your thoughts, feelings, and prayers as you go along.

Honesty Is the Best Policy

1. Open with prayer.

2. Read Psalm 139:23-24. When we dare to talk to God about our feelings—anger, lust, despair, fear—he shines a searchlight into our hearts and enables us to ask, *What darkness in me needs to be brought to light and transformed?* The work of change is never easy. But God's light leads us to repentance. Our feelings are often our first signals that we have some soul work to do: that we're avoiding God, mad at him, hurt, rebellious, or indifferent.

3. If you choose to let yourself feel all your feelings, both pleasant and unpleasant, you will begin to feel more alive. You will have new energy because you are no longer numb. What will you do with the new energy you gain when you stop committing your time and energy to things God did not direct you to do? It's important to think about this because you will have more energy for God's plans for you and more passion for the desires he has planted in your heart.

4. Are there some feelings you may have been holding back or denying, whether they are desirable (such as joy and peace) or undesirable (such as anger and pain)? Consider discussing these with a trusted friend or in your small group if you are comfortable doing so.

5. Can you identify ways God has used your losses and pain to shape your character for his purposes? If you have very deep or fresh wounds, do not try to answer this question today. It may be some time before you are able to see how God is redeeming these experiences in your life. Just sit with God and tell him how you feel today. You may decide to share your feelings with a trusted friend later. But healing takes time, and God waits with you. Hope in him.

> *Hope does not disappoint us, because God has poured out his love into our hearts by the Holy Spirit, whom he has given us.*
>
> Romans 5:5

6. Close in prayer, ending with the prayer of surrender: "Lord, thank you for loving and accepting me. I turn over to you my heart, mind, body, and soul. All that I am belongs to you, through Christ, who loved me and gave himself for me. Amen."

TAKE THE TRUTH WITH YOU

God created me with feelings. Instead of ignoring or denying them, I will learn to accept them and recognize them as signals to think and act responsibly. Today I will talk to God about my feelings and trust him to direct my actions.

Emotional Honesty with God

Emotional honesty is a part of intimacy with God. When we are angry, discouraged, or doubtful, we may hesitate to express our feelings to God because we think we have to shape up and get our attitude in order first. But God wants us to be honest with him, to turn to him and pour out the contents of our hearts as we trust him to help us grow and change. Below are examples of heroes of the faith who were emotionally honest as they spoke with God.

> *"I cry out to you, O God, but you do not answer; I stand up, but you merely look at me. You turn on me ruthlessly; with the*

*might of your hand you attack me. You snatch me up and
drive me before the wind; you toss me about in the storm. I
know you will bring me down to death, to the place appointed
for all the living."* (Job, in Job 30:20-23)

*"I cannot carry all these people by myself; the burden is too
heavy for me. If this is how you are going to treat me, put me
to death right now—if I have found favor in your eyes—and do
not let me face my own ruin."*

(Moses, in Numbers 11:14-15)

*"I am the man who has seen affliction by the rod of his wrath.
He has driven me away and made me walk in darkness rather
than light; indeed, he has turned his hand against me again
and again, all day long."* (Jeremiah, in Lamentations 3:1-3. See
also Lamentations 3:19-23.)

*"Be merciful to me, Lord, for I am faint; O Lord, heal me, for
my bones are in agony. My soul is in anguish. How long,
O Lord, how long? . . . I am worn out from groaning; all night
long I flood my bed with weeping and drench my couch with
tears."* (David, in Psalm 6:2-3, 6)

*"Why, O Lord, do you reject me and hide your face from me?
From my youth I have been afflicted and close to death . . .
and am in despair. Your wrath has swept over me; your terrors
have destroyed me. All day long they surround me like a flood;
they have completely engulfed me. You have taken my
companions and loved ones from me; the darkness is my
closest friend."* (Heman, in Psalm 88:14-18.
See also Psalm 89:1-2)

Notice how Job, Moses, Jeremiah, and David, and Heman freely
express all of their emotions to God. This is part of their intimacy
with him. And God calls them his faithful ones. God is not put off
by our human emotions, though we are not to let them rule over

us. We need to center our thoughts on God. Through the power of his Spirit he eventually changes our feelings. This biblical model is a pattern worth following and is a prescription for sound mental, emotional, and spiritual health.

7

The Power of Letting Go

Transformation of our soul requires that we acknowledge its reality and importance, understand scriptural teachings about it, and take it into the yoke of Jesus, learning from him humility and the abandonment of "outcomes" to God.

—Dallas Willard[1]

THE MYTH: Biblical submission requires that I take responsibility for correcting problems and sinful situations in other people's lives and relationships.

Have you heard the story of the man who fell off a cliff? Clutching the grasses at the edge, he was able to delay his fall.

"Is anyone up there?" the man cried.

"Yes," came the reply.

"Who are you? Why don't you help me?" shouted the man.

"I'm God," said the Voice, "and I will help you. But you must do exactly as I say."

"Okay. What do I have to do?"

"First, let go!"

Whereupon the man called out, "Is anybody *else* up there?"[2]

107

I think we're a lot like this man, especially when we face difficult challenges. We cry out, "God help me!" "Help my child!" "Please heal my marriage!" "Please, God, take away my singleness, and send me someone to marry!"

"I will help you, my child," God reassures us. "Just leave everything in my hands."

We give it to God and breathe a sigh of relief—for a while. But when the outcome isn't what we expected or hoped, we ask, "Is that how you answer, God? What kind of love is that?"

If God calls us to let go of our immediate concerns and deal with an impending crisis or fight a spiritual battle, we tend to whine, "I'm not strong enough. I don't have enough courage, enough talent, enough strength. How can you ask me to let go?"

In God's economy, sometimes we can do more when we have fewer resources of our own. Judges 7 is a good illustration of this principle. Gideon had to face an army that far outnumbered his before he could become the mighty warrior God knew he was. When Gideon took a look at the odds and cried to God for help, God responded by cutting the number of fighting men at Gideon's disposal. That way, when they were victorious over their enemies, they would not be able to boast that their success was the result of their own strength.

> "My thoughts are not your thoughts, neither are your ways my ways," declares the Lord.   Isaiah 55:8

When my sons were small, they began to learn about trusting, letting go, and leaving the outcome in God's hands from the story of Shadrach, Meshach, and Abednego. Daniel's three friends refused to bow down and worship the king's golden image: "If we are thrown into the blazing furnace, the God we serve is able to save us from it, and he will rescue us. . . . But even if he does not, we want you to know, O king, that we will not serve your gods or worship the image of gold you have set up" (Daniel 3:17-18).

Even if he does not? Now that takes grit and raw faith. I admired Shadrach, Meshach, and Abednego too, but as a young mom, I knew very little about trusting God and leaving the outcome to him. Even now, years later, it's sometimes hard to tell whether my trust is centered in God and his faithfulness or in a hidden demand that he pull me out of the heat when I think I can't take it anymore.

Have there been times when you struggled to trust in God, to place your concerns in his hands without trying to take them back? We often think we know how things should turn out, and we can't understand why God doesn't buy into our "insight." Then we want to take back control again. It's so easy to play God ourselves, isn't it?

When it comes to our key relationships, we are often unable to leave the results with God because we aren't really trusting his sovereignty to begin with. But biblical submission means trusting in God's sovereignty over our lives and others', praying for our hearts' desires but leaving the results firmly in God's hands. To do that, we need to remind ourselves that God sees from an infinite, eternal perspective far above what our minds and hearts are capable of.

> *Biblical submission means trusting in God's sovereignty over our lives and others,' praying for our hearts' desires but leaving the results firmly in God's hands.*

Seeking a Higher Perspective

Some time ago my friend Marilyn flew to another state to visit extended family. The turbulent winds of trials had blown into her life, and for several months her heart had been heavy. As the plane took off, Marilyn stared out the window at the cloudy gray gloom that surrounded the plane and matched her own mood. But as she watched, the plane climbed above the clouds and was bathed in sunshine. The clouds, now billowy and white in the sunlight, looked so different from the way they had appeared from the ground. It was like entering a new world.

To submit to God's sovereignty is to seek a perspective higher than the one around us or the one usually visible to us. Although we cannot always see our lives from God's perspective, we can trust him because he reigns in the heavenlies, high above everything that surrounds us. Submitting to his sovereignty helps us to resist the urge to "take back control" when we're disappointed in others, in ourselves, in life. God lives above the storms *and* controls them, even when the gloom threatens to overwhelm us.

Emptied Hands, Filled Hearts

Be filled with the Spirit.   EPHESIANS 5:18

On our honeymoon, Frank and I made our first trip to Eureka Springs, Arkansas, a place we have grown to love. A few miles outside the Springs is the War Eagle Mill, a working gristmill famous for its cornmeal and other milled products. Frank and I watched the large waterwheel turning in the currents of the stream to supply the power needed to operate the mill. As water from the upper level filled the cups attached to the wheel, its weight pushed them downward and turned the wheel. At the bottom, the cups emptied into the stream. The empty cups, now lighter, are carried to the top of the wheel, where they fill with water and repeat the cycle that gives power to the grinding wheel in the mill.

The mill is a picture of what happens as we learn to give up control, accept things that don't conform to our own personal agendas, and admit, "I don't like this, but I will do it God's way." It is part of the daily—and lifelong—process of maturing as a Christian. There's a sort of rhythm to it, a circular flow. Just as the water fills the cups of the waterwheel and supplies power to the mill, God fills us with his Spirit and supplies his power to walk according to his ways. We empty our burden of sins, concerns, expectations, and things we cannot control into his hands, and he fills our emptiness with his truth, comfort, and power. He pours his love down on us, we pour out our concerns into his hands and return empty again and again to be filled and refilled. God is the stream of living water that flows into our spirits and empowers us. He is the caretaker of all we let go of.

Are you struggling to let go of something? Perhaps it's a serious health concern, the state of your finances, or a child intent on following a prodigal path. Many women would say the hardest thing to leave in God's care is their children. I once read a magazine article about a mother's struggle to release control of her eighteen-year-old son, who had started using drugs. As he drove away from their home, the woman knew she could be letting him go into sin, failure, and misery. She fell to her knees and sobbed in desperation, "Lord, what am I doing wrong?"

The answer came to her heart: "All your children will be taught by the Lord."

Is that in the Bible? she wondered. Searching her concordance, she found the words in Isaiah 54:13. God was asking her to get out of the way, to relinquish her control over her child to him. So she wrote a prayer of relinquishment in her journal and asked, "Lord Jesus, help me to be faithful."[3]

Letting Go of Outcomes

Often, the need to leave the lives of our loved ones in God's hands is where letting go gets really tough. We're so accustomed to responding to them, attending to their needs, "fixing their lunches." We cry out, "Hello? God? Is anybody up there?" It's tempting for mothers to want to be "fixers" when things aren't going well for their children—at any age. Like the man who fell off the cliff and was hanging on in desperation, we tend to ask, "Is anybody *else* up there?"

Things may even appear to be going in the opposite direction of how we thought God would do things. But relinquish we must if we want God to do the fixing in his way and in his time. Like the woman in the article, many moms must watch a child walk out the door, get in the car, and drive away. The mothers are left to pace the floor, watch, and pray, just as the father of the Prodigal Son did.

Have you ever wondered what the mother of the Prodigal Son was doing during that prolonged time of agony? I don't know of a mom who has been able to stop fixing things without getting serious about that prayer of relinquishment, pouring out her concerns and heart-aches, letting go of control of her beloved one, and sending her love and care through the holy circuitry of prayer. Others may blame her for her child's addiction, criminal acts, premarital sexual behavior, unwanted pregnancy, or whatever it is that needs fixing. In this, too, she must let go and trust God for direction, or she's likely to get caught in the sticky web of blame and resentment.

Those who must wait on God for the outcome as they let a prodigal go into the world know for sure they don't have the power to make things turn out right. But perseverance today builds strength for tomorrow. In time they realize that in letting go, they have received a great gift—the presence of God's Spirit as they trust in the One who sees everything from above the clouds.

When we leave our problems in God's hands, we don't need to demand outcomes as proof of his love. We will still pray our hearts out on behalf of our children and loved ones—and God may still put us through the fire—but he will come and save us, no matter what. He will do it on *his* terms. If we truly believed this all the time, we would be free to risk, to love, to give everything we have to others without fearing what we may or may not get back in return.

Letting Go of Your Expectations

I scatter to the right and to the left the good seed that the good God puts into my little hand for my little birds. What happens then is its own business. . . . The good God says to me, "Give, give, always give, without bothering yourself at all about the results." —St. Therese of Lisieux[4]

Letting go and trusting God is the opposite of seeking control. When we give and receive freely, our fulfillment comes in giving, serving, and loving rather than in getting what we expect or think we deserve in return. In the movie *Enchanted April,* Lottie and Rose, two proper Englishwomen, give us a glimpse of what it can look like to take a risk without knowing whether you'll get anything in return.

They rent an Italian villa with two other ladies, Mrs. Fisher, a grouchy recluse, and Lady Caroline, an heiress. By splitting expenses four ways, the burned-out, bored, and disillusioned women can afford the getaway, which each woman needs for different reasons but with one common motive: to get away from people.

Rose doesn't understand why her faithfulness and relentless prayers aren't making her life more interesting or stimulating. Lottie also wants an escape from the humdrum boredom of home. In the idyllic seaside setting, all four women settle into the Italian castle for a monthlong vacation.

After only a day or two, Lottie begins to make some surprise discoveries about her disillusionment and decides to invite her husband to join her.

"What? Invite your husband? But I thought you came to get away from him," exclaims Rose.

"The important thing is to have lots of love about," says Lottie. "I was very stingy with it back home. I used to measure and count it out. I had this obsession with justice." In the new setting, Lottie begins to realize she's been blaming her husband for her own boredom, resenting him for her unhappiness, expecting him to be like her instead of valuing the differences between them. Reminiscing with Rose, Lottie muses regretfully, "I wouldn't love him [her husband] unless he loved me back exactly as much. And if he didn't, neither did I. The emptiness of it all."

When Lottie's husband arrives, her sweetness draws his devoted attention like a bee to honeysuckle blossoms. Love blooms anew between the couple, and Lottie encourages Rose to invite her husband too. By this time, Rose is also unwinding—inside and out—loosening the tight bun at the back of her neck and letting her long hair cascade down her back in loose curls.

Dare she dream that love might be rekindled in her own marriage as it has in Lottie's? But she recalls her husband's long absences and preoccupation with his career. *He probably wouldn't come anyway. I bore him,* she thinks. But Rose finally works up the courage to invite her husband, and with time and space to rediscover the little things they love in each other with no expectations, love blooms anew for her and her husband. Before long, all four women and their companions are dropping their guard, ditching their demands that others meet their needs. Instead, they are free to embrace the joy of loving without knowing what they will get back in return.

How often we Christian women measure out our love and good deeds and then calculate what we expect as a payback. But this is not the sort of love that springs forth from the heart at the prompting of the Lord Jesus. It's not the love that takes delight in giving without any thought of what we will receive in return. As Christians, we have it all, but God never meant for us to hold on to what he has freely given us. That only blocks the flow and causes us to become demanding and expect something in return because of what we've given out or given up.

We may *call* this love, but it's not God's kind of love. We may disguise our hidden demand as submission, but it's not submission—to either God, a spouse, an authority figure, or someone else we want to serve. If we are stingy, then like Lottie, we will find our lives bone dry, empty of love and compassion.

Letting Go of Your Treasure

If we're serious about submitting our lives to God, sooner or later it will cost us what we most value. This was something the rich ruler in Luke 18:18-23 could not do:

> Once a religious leader asked Jesus this question: "Good teacher, what should I do to get eternal life?"
>
> "Why do you call me good?" Jesus asked him. "Only God is truly good. But as for your question, you know the commandments: 'Do not commit adultery. Do not murder. Do not steal. Do not testify falsely. Honor your father and mother.'"
>
> The man replied, "I've obeyed all these commandments since I was a child."
>
> "There is still one thing you lack," Jesus said. "Sell all you have and give the money to the poor, and you will have treasure in heaven. Then come, follow me."
>
> But when the man heard this, he became sad because he was very rich. (NLT)

This man had a lot, and that made it hard for him to let go. Those of us who are not rich like the man in Luke 18 may not be able to identify with that, and the idea of delayed gratification doesn't sound so bad when we have a treasure in heaven waiting for us. Yet whether we're rich or poor, young or old, there are always things to which we cling too tightly, as if they actually belong to us instead of to God. What are those things for you? What does Jesus ask us to do with those things? If we're serious about following him, the answer is the same for us as it was for the rich man or for Abraham when God asked him to sacrifice Isaac. We must take the thing we want most *not* to let go of, and lay it on the altar.

Our consolation is the knowledge that God will give us strength equal to what he asks of us. And in ways we cannot understand, arrange, or predict, he will give us back even more than we let go of.

I would be embarrassed to tell you how many times I have discovered that I was making some hidden demand of someone I love, wanting some particular thing in return. But because I have so often rediscovered God's joy in the midst of my ridiculous demands on someone, I want to share just one humorous example.

I had ordered a new pellet gun for Frank's birthday. It was something he wanted, to discourage varmints from munching the wood-shingled roof of our house, and I got the stock number from a friend who already owned a gun like the one Frank wanted.

My birthday was also coming up two and a half weeks before Frank's, but because of unusual stresses at work, Frank was unable to get me a birthday present or even a card, which is not typical for him. I told Frank it was okay, not to worry, that I understood he had been preoccupied. But as my birthday passed unnoticed and Frank's birthday approached, a mean little voice inside me whispered, *Maybe you should return his gift and get your money back. After all, he didn't get you anything!* I realized that even though I was hiding from my true feelings, I was feeling resentful. As days passed, I was tired instead of happy and excited about giving Frank the gift I had selected for him just a few weeks earlier.

"God, I don't like admitting it, but I am resentful," I blurted out sullenly. "I don't like it that I want to be in control and make sure Frank gives me what I think I deserve. But what I don't like even more is that I am robbing myself of the joy of giving Frank his gift." I was not loving Frank in God's way. I was not resting in God's sovereignty or receiving his joy. Although I had purchased a nice gift for my husband, my brand of love was stingy, calculating, and loaded with a hidden demand for justice.

As I reflected on my motives, on Frank's stressed schedule, and on some other pressures in his extended family at the time, I realized I was not making allowance for the circumstances in Frank's life at the time, and *that* was the gift God really wanted me to give. It wasn't something God would demand of me, but it was an opportunity to be deeply blessed if I would let go of my desire for control.

On the morning of Frank's birthday, I got out of bed, collected cards friends and relatives had sent to him during the previous week, and placed them on the kitchen table beside a carton of chocolate milk and a Moon Pie (his favorite snack). The box holding the gun was too large to wrap, so I just stuck a big purple bow on it. Now that God had adjusted my attitude, my happy anticipation of Frank's seeing his birthday surprises was nothing short of what a child feels on Christmas morning, and I experienced the joy that comes from being on the giving end of love.

There are far nobler examples of what we've been talking about here—people who return a blessing for a curse or pray for their persecutors. But whether the example is a mundane one, like mine over Frank's birthday gift, or something more dramatic, such as forgiving the person who killed a loved one, we are able to empty ourselves and be filled again only as we seek Christ's empowering strength day after day.

Letting Go of the Good to Gain the Best

When in God's strength we stop clinging to our own agendas, it becomes easier to let go of grudges, riches, and expectations and become more forgiving and accepting. Instead of pointing the finger of blame at others, we begin to examine our own thoughts and behavior because we are submitting our minds, hearts, and wills to God's greater plan for us.

Over lunch at our favorite tearoom, my friend Alice shared something she learned from the writings of Mother Teresa, who encouraged everybody to be like Jesus even if they don't get the results they want:

> *People are often unreasonable, illogical and self-centered—*
> *   forgive them anyway.*
> *If you are kind, people may accuse you of selfish, ulterior*
> *   motives—be kind anyway.*
> *If you are successful, you will win some false friends and some*
> *   true enemies—succeed anyway.*
> *If you are honest and frank, people may cheat you—be honest*
> *   and frank anyway.*
> *What you spend years building, someone could destroy over-*
> *   night—build anyway.*
> *If you find serenity and happiness, they may be jealous—*
> *   be happy anyway.*
> *The good you do today, people will often forget tomorrow—*
> *   do good anyway.*
> *Give the world your best, and it may never be enough—give the*
> *   world your best anyway.*
> *You see, in the final analysis, it is between you and God.*
> *It was never between you and them anyway.*
>
> *—Mother Teresa[5]*

It is never between us and other people—it's between us and God. That's the point. God wants to fill us with faith, hope, and love. If we are to be filled with his virtues, we must admit our resentment, demands, and expectations and give them up to him. Each day we die little deaths: We give up things we want and gain what God wants for us. A plan or dream of ours dies, but he gives us another one to take its place. Day by day we die to self and become alive to God's greater purposes for us.

The need to let go of earthly concerns will continue until we reach heaven. We trust God because that's the only way we can make it through. But Jesus keeps things turning anyway. If we remember that God gave us the good gifts in the first place, it will be a little easier to let go of those things when it's time. If we can remember that we might not have had those treasures at all, then we will cherish the memories of the blessings we've had, let go of them when we need to, and be on the lookout for new ones God has on the horizon.

It is really only the poor in spirit who can, actually, have anything, because they are the ones who know how to receive gifts. For them, everything is a gift.   —Simon Tugwell[6]

● ● ● ● ● ● ● ● ● ● ● ● ● ● ●

REFLECT ON THE TRUTH

The following questions and exercises are intended to help you prayerfully reflect on what you have read. You might want to use a notebook or journal for writing down your thoughts, feelings, and prayers as you go along.

Control Is No Substitute for Trust

1. Open with prayer.

2. Read Psalm 91:9-16.

3. Think of something you need to let go of. It may be a health concern, financial concern, relationship burden, worry over a child. Write a prayer of relinquishment. Give yourself, your loved ones, your anxieties, your unfinished plans, your dreams to God. When you do this, you can truly rejoice—perhaps not in the trials themselves but in God's nurturing companionship with you in the midst of them. In the end, our trials make us stronger— and more and more his.

4. As Christians, we want to let go of our problems and give them to God, but we cannot do it unless we first accept the feelings that accompany them, including grief, which comes and goes like the ebb and flow of the ocean tide. Throughout the Scriptures we see the pattern of accepting reality, acknowledging our feelings, grieving, letting go of our concerns, and accepting things as they are:

> [Jesus cried out,] "O Jerusalem, Jerusalem, you who kill the prophets and stone those sent to you, how often I have longed to gather your children together, as a hen gathers her chicks under her wings, but you were not willing. Look, your house is left to you desolate. For I tell you, you will not see me again until you say, 'Blessed is he who comes in the name of the Lord.'"
>
> Matthew 23:37-39

Jesus accepted the reality of the problem. He acknowledged that the people did not follow his path. He grieved. He wept over Jerusalem because he knew they would not accept him. There is a point of acceptance of reality and then a point of moving on.

Following Christ's example as we practice facing our problems, grieving when we need to instead of burying our emotions, and being truthful about our circumstances, we become more joyful because we are more convinced that God really is in control.

5. Use the outline on the next page to help you transcend a problem in Christ's strength.

6. Close in prayer, ending with the prayer of surrender: "Lord, thank you for loving and accepting me. I turn over to you my heart, mind, body, and soul. All that I am belongs to you, through Christ, who loved me and gave himself for me. Amen."

TRANSCENDING A PROBLEM IN CHRIST'S STRENGTH

1. What is the problem or issue? Name it.

- I cannot let go of it until I own it.
- I cannot own it until I let myself feel it.
- I cannot feel it until I accept its reality.
- I cannot accept its reality until I forgive with my will. (What do I need to forgive at this time so that I can persevere?)
- I cannot forgive until I surrender my emotions about it to God.
- I cannot surrender my emotions about it until I seek the grace of God to make me better instead of bitter. (Pray for grace. God can heal what I can't.)
- I cannot make use of the grace of God until I remember that I don't have to save the world. That is God's part.

2. Commit to transcending the problem in Christ's strength:

- I will trust God to make me strong enough to transcend this problem.
- I will call on God's grace to help me endure.
- Because of God's grace, I will accept the reality of this problem. I will admit it is true.
- I will honestly surrender my emotions to God, whatever they are. I will acknowledge and name my feelings to him.
- I will choose with my will *to forgive*.

- I will let myself feel the pain that results because of this problem. I will continue forgiving with my will and admitting my real feelings to God. He understands. In time, he will change my emotions. In the meantime, I will keep trusting him.
- I will let go of the concern and place it in God's hands. I will not take it back. I will let go of the outcome. If I take it back, I will repeat the process until I truly leave the outcome in God's hands.
- I will accept what is, because God is in control.
- I will thank God because by his grace, in the name of Jesus Christ, I am strengthened to transcend this problem.

When a new problem arises, go through these steps prayerfully. If you write your thoughts in a journal, you can look back and see how God is healing you and helping you to grow in his grace and making you stronger in your inner woman for his glory.

TAKE THE TRUTH WITH YOU

Biblical submission means trusting in God's sovereignty. It is God's job to fix people, problems, and relationships. My job is to live truthfully, keeping things out in the open and leaving the outcome in God's hands.

8

Embracing Your Humanness

*Those who don't have anything to prove or protect can
believe they are loved as they are.* —Richard Rohr[1]

THE MYTH: If I submit myself to God, I will overcome all my weaknesses and flaws.

Some time ago I drove to the local Merle Norman store for some
makeup. I wanted a new lipstick for summer, so I asked the store
attendant to help me select one. She brushed on a sample of
lipstick and placed a lighted mirror in front of me.

"How do you like it?" she asked. I nearly gasped. Not only was
the mirror lighted; it also magnified everything. Every pore looked
like an ant hole, and I saw facial flaws I didn't know I had.

"The lipstick is fine," I said, chuckling, "but you can keep that
mirror!"

Most of us don't like magnifying mirrors, especially if we're over
thirty-five. It's hard to see ourselves as we really are, whether
we're looking at the outside or the inside. But trying *not* to see
what lies within makes it harder for us to see our humanness and
to recognize the lavish graciousness of God, who loves us as his

one-of-a-kind creations. He wants us to accept ourselves as he accepts us—strengths, irregularities, flaws—the whole package.

Sometimes our thinking gets off track, and we begin believing that if we submit to God and obey the Scriptures, we'll get rid of our weaknesses, problems, and flaws, because God doesn't want us to have them. We may start to deny our faults and problems and hide our uniqueness because we think they keep us from being perfect. But this isn't what Jesus meant when he said, "Be perfect, therefore, as your heavenly Father is perfect" (Matthew 5:48).

Here, *perfect* means developing, growing in maturity as God's woman. God wants us to submit all that we are to him. A weakness, a problem, an irregular way of serving him, may be the thing Christ uses to glorify him most. God is able to redeem *all* things for his glory. But we can submit to God only those things that we first accept in ourselves.

Everything we reject or deny remains outside the realm of what we can surrender to him because we are so busy ignoring it. Let's say we have a gift, or a flaw, that we don't want to have, perhaps a sickness, such as fibromyalgia, or wealth we don't enjoy managing or a temperament that doesn't seem to fit the vocation we think God wants us to pursue. When we give it to God, he may turn it into *the very quality* he will shine most brightly through. Through these windows into our souls, someone else may get a look at Jesus they desperately need as they see what God has done in us. As we submit all that we are to God, we are free to serve others without being preoccupied with our imperfections, faults, differences, or our own agendas. This is authentic dying to self.

This is not easy to do, but I believe it is a gift of God's grace as we experience his love day after day. It happens as we get comfortable with ourselves and offer ourselves for Christ's glory, even if we don't fit the mold that our culture—even our Christian culture—may have defined as normal.

Embracing Your Uniqueness

Have you seen Rodgers and Hammerstein's *The Sound of Music*? It is rich in imagery and gives us a picture of a woman who learns to submit to God and trust him for direction as she holds on to her uniqueness in any setting.

"What is the most important lesson you've learned here?" the Mother Abbess asks Maria near the beginning of the movie.

"To find out what is the will of God and do it wholeheartedly," Maria replies without hesitation. Maria loves God and wants with all her heart to fulfill God's purpose for her life. She thinks this means becoming a nun, but she can't seem to find space in her life for the structure and order required for living at the abbey. Maria doesn't fit the stereotype of a nun. Instead of being quiet, meditative, serious, and structured, she's spontaneous and lighthearted and loves nature, music, and children. Yet she believes it is God's will that she stay at the abbey.

The Mother Abbess isn't so sure and sends Maria to the home of Captain von Trapp as a governess to his seven children in hopes that it will help Maria learn God's will for her future. Maria blows into the von Trapp household on wings of change and doesn't fit as a governess either; in fact, she's as different from other governesses as she is from the other nuns at the abbey. But she wins the children's affection by doing what comes naturally: teaching them to sing, play, have courage, and face their problems with a positive attitude. Maria repeatedly gets into trouble by being late, breaking house rules for the children, and even defending the children's behavior to their father. She's also falling in love with the captain.

Maria returns to the abbey to seek further direction from God. There, as she renews her faith in God and reaffirms her primary role as his servant, her love for the captain settles into a more peaceful place in her heart, and after some time, she is happily reunited with the von Trapps—confident, secure in her role as governess, appropriate in her relationship with the captain.

But by this time the captain has fallen in love with Maria. He had missed her spirit, wit, and humor, her boldness, spontaneity, and love of life—even though they are not qualities common to governesses or to women he would normally consider marrying. God's direction becomes crystal clear for Maria, Captain von Trapp, and his children: They are to become a family.

When we submit all that we are to God—our strengths, weaknesses, irregularities, or our worst flaws—in time, our submission yields something much larger than ourselves, something that brings glory to Christ.

As Maria held on to all that was different in herself and sought the will of God, he faithfully directed her path. God didn't ask her to rearrange herself, to give up her unique qualities. He worked through Maria as she was to bring glory to Christ. You may be searching for God's will and long to do it wholeheartedly. You don't have to be perfect or have the same qualities you admire in someone else. God accepts you as you are, and he wants you to accept yourself as you are and to give yourself to him. He will help you grow in maturity in his way and in his time.

God gives gifts to his children at his own discretion. Sometimes it's a bit irregular, as when he called Deborah to serve as a judge in Israel in Judges 4. Or consider Anne Graham Lotz's calling as a minister. Part of dying to self is responding to God's call and surrendering all that we are to him.

Think about some of the obstacles in your past, things that may have hurt you, or ways you are different from others. God is using these to make you stronger, to grow and mature you, to make you perfect on his terms. We jump in and take a stab at what we think God is guiding us to do, and under his guidance, we go on from there. When we submit all that we are to God—our strengths, weaknesses, irregularities, or our worst flaws—in time, our submission yields something much larger than ourselves, something that brings glory to Christ.

Embracing Your Weaknesses

I thank God for my handicaps, for, through them, I have found myself, my work and my God. —Helen Keller[2]

If accepting our strengths is sometimes hard because it requires that we stretch, grow, and become more like Christ, accepting our weaknesses and flaws can also be challenging. We may have trouble understanding that God really isn't interested in shining us up and putting us on display for others to admire. He wants others to see him through our lives, just as we are. This requires that we tell the truth about ourselves, admit our flaws, and stay close to him. God can use even our most glaring struggles to show his power and glory if we are willing to submit those struggles to him.

I was surprised to learn that Charles Haddon Spurgeon, the "prince of preachers," suffered with depression throughout his life. Although I have faced depression in my own life, I guess I thought great preachers would somehow be exempt. If you have also suffered with an area of emotional vulnerability, be encouraged. Others before us have glorified God and helped others draw closer to him as they submitted their imperfect lives and struggles to his care.

Richard Day, one of Spurgeon's biographers, refused to gloss over the preacher's episodes of depression. He saw it as an opportunity to highlight the sweet release God gave Spurgeon at the end of his low times, in which he exhibited "such radiant new love for his Redeemer. . . . Spurgeon was weak, yet strong. Ill, yet triumphant. He had emotional problems, but they only refined him into the finest of gold which bore the image of that Great Refiner of souls." Thus, an onset of depression became to him "a prophet in rough clothing," heralding the coming of a larger blessing for those he ministered to, as the glory of Christ was demonstrated through Spurgeon's submitted emotional pain.[3]

What a radical thought: to expect *a blessing for others* to result from one's own emotional distress instead of remaining obsessed, as most of us do, with being well and on top of things. How different Spurgeon's attitude toward his affliction is from our rejection of emotional struggles and pain as something that repels God.

We do not get to choose the means God will use to show himself through us, whether it be strength, weakness, or more likely—at least to those who know us well—a combination of both. As we learn to accept ourselves the way God accepts us—as imperfect human beings saved by grace—we become more yielded servants, available to reflect his glory in whatever way he chooses.

Embracing Your Helplessness

> *We must learn the art of weakness, of non-achievement, of being able to cope with the knowledge of our own poverty and helplessness, without trying to escape from it into something we can accept more easily.* —Simon Tugwell[4]

The ups and downs of life allow us opportunities to find ourselves recipients of our heavenly Father's love over and over again. This makes it worth the bumps and bruises we accumulate along the way. In *The Shaking of the Foundations*, German theologian Paul Tillich writes, "Do not seek for anything, do not perform anything, do not intend anything. Simply accept the fact that you are accepted."[5]

How are you doing at simply accepting the fact that you are

accepted? Perhaps you're aware of your strengths and uniqueness—you're offering them in service to God and others. You're also aware of your weaknesses, and you're trusting him to work through them, too. Yet perhaps a lingering splinter of bitterness remains, or maybe nagging guilt over something from the past (perhaps far in the past) keeps pulling at the coattails of your soul.

Sometimes the most difficult part of accepting ourselves is accepting our utter helplessness. Perhaps something happened that was out of our control, yet we think that if we had been more alert, more devout, it wouldn't have happened. In such cases, before we can accept ourselves as God accepts us, we may need to forgive ourselves. Although this idea may strike you as strange, think about it. If we have been holding a grudge against ourselves for falling short, self-forgiveness is just what we need. Unless we forgive ourselves for being human and helpless against many of life's circumstances, we will hold ourselves back from embracing God's grace and find ourselves blocked from loving others as God loves us.

Jody was in her midfifties when I first met her. In our women's group, she often talked about times she and her husband shared with her grown son and his wife and their four-year-old granddaughter, whom she often babysat. As we met for coffee one day, Jody stared out the glass storefront as rain pelted the sidewalk.

"There's something I want to tell you," she said quietly. "I used to have a daughter."

Caught off guard by Jody's comment, I waited for her to continue, but she didn't.

"A daughter?" I asked awkwardly.

"Yes. Her name was Claudia. She was seventeen when she killed herself," Jody said as tears brimmed her eyes. Jody said that just one week before her daughter's high school graduation, Claudia asphyxiated herself in their family car as it was parked in the garage.

"As a family, we've talked about Claudia's death at times. We try to remember her on special occasions and holidays when we're together. The grief group we attended together helped us accept our feelings and forgive her for leaving us. But I'll never forgive myself for letting it happen. Even Marcy [her granddaughter] knows she had an Auntie Claudia at one time, and I told her Claudia's 'accident' was my fault. After all, what kind of mother lets her daughter kill herself?"

Over the next few weeks, Jody and I talked several times, and she agreed to see a counselor. Although Claudia's death had occurred almost twenty years earlier and Jody had worked through a lot of her grief and pain, she still held a bitter grudge against herself because of her daughter's suicide. Time passed, and I saw Jody occasionally in our women's group. Then one day she phoned, and there was a note of joy in her voice. She had some news to share, and we made plans to get together.

From the table at the restaurant I saw Jody and her granddaughter, Marcy, coming to join me. I adjusted my expectations to a lighter time together that day, doubting that Jody would discuss Claudia's suicide with a child present.

After we ordered lunch, Jody told me about a lesson she and Marcy had been learning together: Marcy had recently turned five, and she had been delighted with her grandmother's gift, a porcelain tea set she had been hoping for. Marcy had set the tea set on the floor beside her and continued unwrapping her other presents. Somehow, in all the excitement, she had tripped and shattered the teapot.

"It's okay, Marcy," Jody had soothed, trying to comfort her wailing granddaughter. "It was an accident. You didn't mean to break it."

"No, Grandmother," Marcy had protested. "It's *not* okay."
Puzzled, Jody stared at her granddaughter as she explained

between sobs. "Accidents are *not* okay. It's your fault that Aunt Claudia died, and it's my fault that my tea set got broken!"

As Jody finished telling this story, I was picturing her kneeling down to embrace her granddaughter as they wept together, each grieving the loss of something precious and recognizing the need to forgive themselves and accept the reality of things beyond their control. Though it had been far beyond little Marcy's ability to comprehend, her five-year-old logic had clarified a grown-up point, finally breaking through the grudge Jody had been holding against herself for nearly two decades.

Broken tea sets and broken lives result in healthy grief. We lose things and people we love; God comforts, forgives, and accepts us as we are. In his strength we can do the same. We can accept ourselves, even when we are helpless to stop something we didn't want to happen. We're just imperfect women, facing life as it comes. Only God is in control.

Let's not waste time and energy trying to ignore our strengths because we don't want to develop them. Let's not waste time and energy punishing ourselves because we can't get rid of our flaws, or holding grudges against ourselves because we couldn't stop a disaster or because we've made mistakes. Jesus wants us to accept ourselves as his beloved children—no more and no less valuable than any of his others.

When we accept ourselves as God accepts us, we will be free to love others as he has loved us because we will have learned from him how to do it.

[Jesus said,] "You are the light of the world—like a city on a mountain, glowing in the night for all to see. Don't hide your light under a basket! Instead, put it on a stand and let it shine for all."

MATTHEW 5:14-15, NLT

REFLECT ON THE TRUTH

The following questions and exercises are intended to help you prayerfully reflect on what you have read. You might want to use a notebook or journal for writing down your thoughts, feelings, and prayers as you go along.

You Are Who You Are

1. Open with prayer.

2. Read Psalm 92.

3. In *The Sound of Music*, Maria wanted to know the will of God for her life and do it wholeheartedly. Yet in every setting, whether at the abbey in the role of nun or at the von Trapp home in the role of governess, she was a bit "irregular." Do you ever find it difficult to accept ways you are irregular or different (without being in violation of God's ways)?

4. Is there something you need to forgive in yourself or in another person: a grudge against yourself? bitterness toward someone who has hurt you? resentment toward God for letting it happen? We need to forgive so that we can continue to grow in our faith.

5. You may have heard that it helps to forgive an offender by writing a letter (though usually not sending it) that acknowledges your pain, releases your anger, and helps you move toward forgiveness. Perhaps you have written such a letter yourself. But if the pain and confusion still linger, try "sitting down outside yourself," seeing yourself as one of God's dear children in need of love and forgiveness. Would you treat a friend as harshly as you are treating yourself?

Using your own words, write a letter of forgiveness to yourself. Here is a sample to help you get started:

Dear Jody,

I am writing to say I'm sorry for hurting you. I'm sorry for blaming you because you did not stop your daughter's suicide. I regret holding a grudge against you all these years when you had no way of knowing your daughter was going to do what she did. I realize that by rejecting and blaming you, I blocked God's healing process, so it took much longer. I now know that God understands the struggle to forgive and does not expect us to do it quickly when wounds are deep. He understands that we need to grieve. I am sorry that you still live with the pain of losing your daughter, and I'm sorry for blaming you for it. I wish that I had been more compassionate.

Jody, I cannot change yesterday. But I can show compassion today by accepting you as you are and by letting God bring about healing on his terms. Today I will embrace you as you are.

Romans 8:1-2 says, "There is now no condemnation for those who are in Christ Jesus, because through Christ Jesus the law of the Spirit of life set me free from the law of sin and death." Thank God that you are not under condemnation, not even your own!

6. Close in prayer, ending with the prayer of surrender: "Lord, thank you for loving and accepting me. I turn over to you my heart, mind, body, and soul. All that I am belongs to you through Christ, who loved me and gave himself for me. Amen."

TAKE THE TRUTH WITH YOU

God wants me to accept myself as he does—uniquenesses, flaws, and all. As I submit all that I am to him, he demonstrates his strength through my weakness, my problems, and my irregularities, and his glory shines through me.

PART
THREE

Dying to Self
and
Becoming Alive to God

Mercy is no soft option. It is not a matter
of conniving or finding excuses. It is the
only really hard-headed response to evil,
faced frankly and judged accurately for
what it is. It is the only power which can
face evil and not flinch, because it knows a
power stronger than evil, the power of
God's Word, in which the promise of
creation still stands, and in which, therefore, the seed of new creation waits to
germinate.

—Simon Tugwell[1]

9

The Joy of True Submission

We do not lose heart. Though outwardly we are wasting away, yet inwardly we are being renewed day by day.   2 CORINTHIANS 4:16

THE MYTH: If God takes from me what is most precious, I must be cursed instead of blessed.

The first time I watched the film *I Dreamed of Africa,* I was moved by the courageous spirit of Kuki Gallman, who left the safety of family and home in Italy to search out the adventure of a lifetime in Africa.

I sensed the story held some hidden message for me, so I bought the book, trying to glean the goody it offered about the meaning of life, service to a cause greater than ourselves, and what it may cost us.

The thing about Kuki that intrigued me most was her enchantment with and devotion to the continent of Africa itself. Before her father died, he had told her stories about the land's dangers, its people, and their political causes. As Kuki grew up, her father scattered seeds of curiosity across the soil of her youthful mind, and by the time she experienced Africa for herself as a teenager, it was as if she already knew and loved the people and its creatures.

Africa gave many good gifts to Kuki, but it also took its toll on her. Near the end of Kuki's pregnancy with her daughter, her husband, Paolo, was hit by a truck and died. Three years later Kuki's seventeen-year-old son, Emanuele, was killed by a viper as he was extracting venom to prepare serum. Relatives from Italy begged Kuki to return home with them to raise her little daughter in a place of safety. Her mother and sister thought Kuki was putting her desire to remain in Africa ahead of her daughter's need for security.

But Kuki was already home. The essence of who she was as a woman had not been endangered or diminished because of what Africa had taken from her. Instead, her life's purpose became clear as she submitted ungrudgingly to the land she belonged to in spite of all it took from her.

"Africa gave us an extraordinary life," Kuki declared during the closing scenes of the film. "Then Africa claimed an extraordinary price. That was Africa's privilege."

Submitting to God's Sovereignty

Kuki's statement in the previous paragraph parallels somewhat an important spiritual truth: For Christians, the source of true joy is submitting ungrudgingly to the sovereign Lord we belong to. As we abandon ourselves to him, he gives us an unpredictable, extraordinary life (though sometimes we would perhaps prefer more predictable and ordinary). With him, we are home where we belong. He lavishes undeserved gifts and unlimited love on us.

As we offer God the highest place of priority in our lives, the Holy Spirit gradually, mysteriously clarifies our purpose in life and keeps our spirits free. God has given himself to us through his

Son, Jesus Christ. It is our privilege to serve him. It is his privilege to give *and take* from us at his discretion.

It won't always be easy to put his glory above everything else in our lives or to give up what he asks of us. But as we fix our eyes on Jesus and on God's Word and try again when we fail, he will claim our hearts inch by inch, the way Africa claimed Kuki Gallman's. Gradually, Christ will take his place at the center of our being, cutting away everything that does not look like him. At times we may not understand how this could possibly be a blessing. We may even think that if we have struggles and problems in our lives and relationships, we must be cursed instead of blessed because God is taking from us what we consider most precious.

Dear sisters, this is not true. If we have come to God by faith in Christ, we are blessed—not cursed—no matter what happens to us in this life. God's blessing comes to us on his own terms. It leads to dying to self and growing stronger in the inner woman. As we persevere in submitting to God ungrudgingly, we will gradually absorb the qualities of Christ's character. We will begin to see that the real blessings of this life are the blessings of what is of Christ—what is spiritual.

> God's blessing comes to us on his own terms. It leads to dying to self and growing stronger in the inner woman.

Everything else that we may have thought so important begins to pale in comparison to becoming like him. He won't announce, "Now hear this: I am getting ready to build into you the quality of discernment [or integrity or loyalty]." Rather, he lovingly chisels that quality into us as he removes what isn't like it. Over time, we begin to see the work he has been doing in our hearts, making us a little more like Jesus. Since it was his work and not ours, we don't take credit for it but are free to enjoy it and share it with others.

As time passes, we begin to see that his undying affection for us, which none of our words, thoughts, feelings, or behaviors can alter, is transforming us through his grace. The only response we can give back is a grateful heart. It seems such a small offering to us. But it is what he wanted most from us all along.

Participating in the Process

If our transformation is the result of the Spirit's work in us, what can we do to participate in the process of our dying to self? We can practice what some call the spiritual disciplines: reading the Scriptures so that we know and remember the ways of God; praying; being part of a church where we can share our joys, gifts, and life's burdens with others; practicing his presence.

As we read God's Word, we absorb his truth and his ways. We learn the right ways to interact with people in our families and in community. In prayer, our relationship with God as our Father becomes a reality to us. We realize that we have a parent who has always loved us. We have a parent who nurtures us day by day and gives us wise guidance, who looks into our faces and smiles, and who delights in us the way we all long to be delighted in.

In prayer we practice a meaningful, interactive, life-changing relationship with Christ.[1] In prayer we submit ourselves to God as our highest priority. As we guard that "inner sanctum" for him first, our other priorities in marriage, friendships, churches, and other circles of influence fall into place. Only then do we have anything of eternal value to give to others. This holy space inside us that we reserve for prayer belongs to Christ. It is his home for the duration of our lives on earth. Here, the Holy Spirit meets with our true self.

In prayer God blesses us with his presence. He offers his

comfort when something precious is taken from us or when we choose to give up something we want in order to please him. In prayer he gives us grace to persevere. And while we are spending time with him, he is claiming us more and more as his own. He is making us into a gift to be passed on to others around us.

Blessing Those Who Persecute You

> We who are alive are always being given over to death
> for Jesus' sake, so that his life may be revealed in our
> mortal body.   2 CORINTHIANS 4:11

I was meeting with a group of intimate Christian friends, and our leader, Iris Pearce, was talking about how God restores and empowers us with his grace. "Grace is the love of God that empowers the soul to do what it needs to do for God, self, and others. It is like mother's milk—it turns into whatever the body needs, whether it's strong bones, teeth, hair, whatever it needs to grow at that time."

After Iris's talk, one of the women told about how God's grace empowered her when a man she had known and trusted did something very harmful to her son.

Linda (not her real name), a mature and devoted Christian, had been focusing on God's mercy over the years as she prayed. When a man did something evil to her son, she began to pray for her son's offender even though in hurting her son, the man had also hurt her. When Linda was reminded of the man's evil, she intensified her prayers, focusing on how the same God who had reached out to pull *her* back from cliffs of destruction when she didn't deserve it also loved the man who had wronged her son.

Linda had drawn an illustration in which she was kneeling in prayer, focusing intently on Christ while the man stabbed her in the back. As we listened to her explanation of the drawing, sighs, groans, and a couple of nervous giggles echoed from different places in the room. But I doubt any of us missed the deeper message of how Linda was able to pray for her son's offender. Because her greatest submission was to God and she was aware of his care, sovereignty, and mercy, he graciously empowered her to be merciful to the offender.

Somebody may have done evil to us, but that's not the *whole* truth. The other part of the truth—more hidden from us but also closer to the ultimate truth—is that God is faithfully at work in our lives behind the scenes. He is building Christ's character into us and giving us opportunities to acknowledge his position at the center of our lives as we lay aside our own priorities and gradually die to self.

With God as the focus of our submission, we become free of preoccupations with our own agendas and free of anxiety when others try to impose their plans on us ahead of our priorities. We can forgive people who try to use others to meet their own needs and demand what others do not have to give instead of trusting God. It's not that they are not responsible for their actions. But we realize that their problems belong to them. The decision about whether we will focus on their part or our part belongs to us. By God's grace, we will decide to concentrate on the part we can do something about—*our* part—and this leads us to dying to self.

In *A Chance to Die*, Elisabeth Elliot writes:

> As we walk through our common duties in the company of Jesus we learn what the taking up of the cross is all about. In what we thought of as our strong point, we find unsuspected weakness—a chance to die! In what we felt quite adequate to perform we discover that we need help—perhaps from someone we thought of as our inferior—another chance to

die! It is an unsettling business, this being made conformable to His death, and it cannot be accomplished without knocking out the props. If we understand that God is at work even when He knocks out the small props, it will not be so difficult for us to take when He knocks out the bigger ones.[2]

God Gives and God Takes Away

In *Talks of Instruction,* Meister Eckhart writes: "God gives no gift, God never has given any gift, in order that anyone should have the gift and rest content with it. Rather, all the gifts that he has ever given, in heaven and on earth, were given in view of his single purpose, to give *one* gift, which is himself."[3]

What gift is God offering you? Perhaps you are like Linda, and God is lovingly—and sometimes painfully—chiseling into you the gift of mercy. It's not always easy to recognize the work of the Holy Spirit in us because we are so attuned to the values of this world. We need spiritual eyes to see Christ at work in this world. He stands ready to give the gifts we *really* need, even though we may never have had the wisdom to ask for them. What woman would not like to become patient, forgiving, and tenderhearted? Yet who would ever order from a catalog the hard lessons it may take to gain these attributes? When we receive ungrudgingly what God gives to us and offer willingly what he takes from us, he gives us something of eternal value that will benefit others, but sometimes it takes us a long time to catch on.

You may have guessed from stories I've told about my dad that I had a lot of admiration for him. He was kind, just, nature-loving, and strict and had lots of other good qualities. I have learned that it's hard for parents of two siblings of the same gender to appreciate and foster each child's uniqueness without doing a lot of comparing. When I was growing up, I felt as if people were comparing me to my only sister. Jan and I were different. She was outgoing, creative, happy, and successful at almost everything she tried. I was reflective, loved music, dancing, and writing, and was sometimes melancholy. Yet my dad could see the best in both my sister and me, and he encouraged uniqueness in each of us, appreciating each of us for the qualities we had.

How devastating it was to find out Daddy had cancer when he was only fifty-seven, and I was twenty-five. By the time we found out, the disease had already spread throughout his body. I'd been a Christian for only two years, and I remember pleading with God for my dad's life. How could God take him away when I was so young? I couldn't bear the thought of my two preschool sons never knowing their grandfather. I couldn't imagine life without him. The timing of this illness was all wrong—I could see that— why couldn't God see it? I was a Christian, but I felt cursed instead of blessed.

The cancer took Daddy's life within five months. Suddenly, all we had left were lots of fond memories, a few tokens to remember him by, and stories—lots of stories.

Because there was no other way for my sons to know my dad or to keep his memory alive, I started writing down our family stories and reading them to my sons on Christmas mornings. After a few years, it became a part of our holiday tradition. As young men, Scott and Brent could appreciate learning about my dad's character, his hobbies and pastimes, and what they had in common with him: Scott's love of golf, fishing, and collecting things and Brent's love of hunting, fishing, gardening, and dogs. I began to see that the gifts my dad had given to people around him were still alive—still enriching us. Even though he had been taken away from us before my sons ever really knew him, traits of his character had been passed down to them, and now we remembered him together as a family through stories.

I also passed down some of Dad's personal trinkets and belongings each year—old watches, hunting knives, silver dollars, and reproductions of old family photos. Scott and Brent did not have the privilege of knowing my dad and sharing experiences with him, but his life is still a blessing to them. And although losing him when my kids were babies once felt like a curse, it turned out not to be. Rather, it was one of those mysteries I would never understand. I could only acknowledge that it was God's privilege to take Daddy when it was time, according to his plan. I'd been given the gift of being his daughter. Now it was my privilege to share him with my sons in the only way I could.

> [Jesus said,] "You're blessed when you feel you've lost what is most dear to you. Only then can you be embraced by the One most dear to you."
>
> MATTHEW 5:4, *THE MESSAGE*

God's Mercy Makes Us Merciful

It has taken me some years to learn that we're very fortunate if we grow up feeling close to even one of our parents. When I was growing up, my mother and I were not very close. I remember feeling lonely and wanting to spend time with her. Mother worked at the grocery store in our hometown of Arvin, California. She worked six days a week, and by the time I was five years old, I knew how to peel potatoes and fry them for dinner. My older sister had other duties to accomplish before Mother got home at seven o'clock in the evening.

On Saturday mornings my sister and I polished the furniture and dusted and vacuumed to keep our house on Plumtree Drive looking its best. I recall polishing our bookcases and wishing Mother and I could just sit down together and read a story from the crisp new set of *Encyclopedia Britannica* she bought us. But she was busy, even when she was at home. For a long time I begrudged her for what she did not give me—her time. I felt cursed—not blessed—even though I was now a Christian. It seemed I'd been robbed of what was precious to so many of my friends—a close relationship with their moms. I tried to get over the hurt, to move past the wound of feeling motherless. But nothing filled the void.

Then one day when I was in the throes of a midlife crisis, God's Spirit convinced me that it was all okay. In just a few seconds his divine presence made up for all I'd been lacking with my mother in years past. In that moment I knew that I was deeply loved, that I always had been, and that nothing could ever change that. Once I realized it was God who was my sovereign authority, the One who determined my worth, who sent me the blessings I *really* needed, who gave me the mother and father I was supposed to have, I was free to give up the grudge. God had been merciful to me, and I wanted to pass on that mercy to others, even—and especially—my mother. It would take time for patterns of woundedness in me to change, but God had changed my heart toward her.

I started remembering all the ways Mother had blessed my sister and me. She had grown up during the Depression, when there were no good jobs to be had and going to bed hungry was not uncommon. I thought of how proud she must have felt that the food pantry in our home was always full, that she could help give my sister and me clothes, toys, family vacations, and a nice house. She had never had these things, and she wanted us to have them. It was as if God opened my eyes so that I could see my mother in a new way, and for this blessing I was grateful.

Mother always made fried apricot pies on New Year's Day, and we ate them while we watched the Rose Parade, but we didn't get much down time with her. I think she must have been delighted when, a generation down the line, she finally had some spare time to spend with my sons, her grandchildren, instead of working full-time.

Now it was time to start writing down the stories about the blessings my mother had passed down to all of us and reading them to my children on Christmas morning. God had given me the mother he wanted me to have, and at last I could be grateful. She lived to be eighty-three, and we shared good times together before she died. At her funeral, I placed two roses on her breast before the casket was closed. A red rose for the gift of life she'd given to me. And a white rose for her own beauty as a woman.

It can take a long time to recognize the blessings God sends to us because often they don't come in the ways we would expect. We tend to look for tangible, visible evidence of blessings in recognizable forms while God is tenderly chiseling away at our characters and lovingly purifying our hearts. He gives us what we *really* need, sometimes withholding what we want most and making sure we can't figure it all out so that we learn to trust him. This is his privilege. His ways are mysterious to us, and that's part of what makes life with him intriguing. He is our sovereign Lord.

Year by year, inch by inch, he is claiming our hearts and turning us into bond servants. He gives and he takes away. This, too, is his privilege because he is our loving Father. It is our privilege to give our lives back to him in service to him and to others.

> Once you were not a people, but now you are the
> people of God; once you had not received mercy, but
> now you have received mercy.   1 PETER 2:10

REFLECT ON THE TRUTH

The following questions and exercises are intended to help you prayerfully reflect on what you have read. You might want to use a notebook or journal for writing down your thoughts, feelings, and prayers as you go along.

The Glad Choice of Surrender

1. Open with prayer.

2. Read Psalm 138:1-3.

3. Throughout your life as a Christian, God is claiming you for himself and chipping away at what is not like him, even when that thing is something you want. How is God claiming you for himself?

4. Have you discovered a defect (such as pride, idolatry, jealousy, lust, or greed) that God is chipping away in you? If so, are you able to thank God for taking something away even if it was something you really wanted? Are you able to tell God that you don't understand but will trust him anyway because he knows best?

5. Have you discovered a virtue (such as hope, faith, or love) that God is building into you? How is he doing that? Thank him for the blessing of virtue, and rejoice in the opportunity to become a little more like Jesus.

6. Close in prayer, ending with the prayer of surrender: "Lord, thank you for loving and accepting me. I turn over to you my heart, mind, body, and soul. All that I am belongs to you, through Christ, who loved me and gave himself for me. Amen."

TAKE THE TRUTH WITH YOU

The source of true joy is submitting ourselves ungrudgingly to the One who knows best. It is his privilege to give and to take from me because he is my loving Father. It is my privilege to serve him.

10

The Freedom of Self-Giving

We are God's workmanship, created in Christ Jesus to
do good works, *which God prepared in advance for us
to do.* EPHESIANS 2:10 (emphasis added)

**THE MYTH: I must make sure my resources are
enough for what God calls me to do. My adequacy
shows I am worthy of God's blessing.**

She was near the town gate at Zarephath when Elijah saw her. He
must have been hungry and thirsty after the ravens stopped
providing food and the brook dried up. Elijah was Israel's most
famous prophet, and I know he was on a mission, but don't you
think he had a lot of nerve, asking that poor widow to scrape the
bottom of her flour jar and bake a cake for him when he knew
that would leave none for her son? Even more, what about the
nerve of the widow, in actually doing as Elijah asked?

This story from 1 Kings 17 reminds me that the widow at
Zarephath was at a place in her faith journey that I have not yet
reached. But it gives me something to look forward to. She must

have had a solid sense that God was in it when Elijah told her, "This is what the Lord, the God of Israel, says: 'The jar of flour will not be used up and the jug of oil will not run dry until the day the Lord gives rain on the land'" (v. 14). It *had* to be God she was believing in and submitting to—not just a wise prophet—because as every mother knows, taking the food out of your hungry child's mouth and giving it to someone else would be horribly difficult. But sure enough, after the widow did as Elijah told her, there was food every day for Elijah, the woman, and her son.

A little later the widow's son became ill and stopped breathing. She must have wondered, *Did God give us life, only to now bring my son's death in this way because I am sinful?* Only after Elijah took the boy's lifeless body and pleaded with God to revive him was the widow all-out convinced that God had surely sent the prophet to them: "Now I know that you are a man of God and that the word of the Lord from your mouth is the truth" (v. 24). All along, this woman's submission was to God, first and last. Out of her deep reverence for him and her desire to serve him, she served others, such as Elijah. As a result, God spared not only the widow's son but also many others.

In some ways we're a lot like the widow. As we submit our hearts to God above everything and everyone else, a desire to serve and give to others flows out of that submission. It's reassuring to remember that the Lord does not ask us to give more than he supplies, even when we've already scraped the bottom of our own resources. We don't have to agonize when others ask something of us for which we do not have the resources. God does not expect us to give what he does not supply.

But sometimes in our attempts to be faithful to God we end up with a problem instead of what we might have expected from God in return for our faithfulness. This is what happened to the widow of Zarephath. At such times it helps to remember we're not at the end of the story yet. As Christians, we walk in the freedom that comes from giving of ourselves day by day, knowing that whatever happens in the meantime, the end of our life story is heaven. We keep our freedom by remembering that only God knows what we may have to bear for his sake, that we can trust him to provide the resources to bear it, and that the Holy Spirit will help us to be okay with that. This keeps things simple, especially when we face unexpected problems.

Submission Is a Process

> [Peter answered,] "We must obey God rather than men!"　　　　　　　　　　　　ACTS 5:29

Frank and I have a friend (I'll call her Sally) whose dad works in a ministry overseas. Some time ago it was discovered that while Sally's dad was serving abroad, he was also taking advantage of young women in that country. The report of the scandal involving priests in Boston hit the newspapers about the same time Sally found out about her father, and she could hardly bear the thought that someone in her family had done the same thing that was now making headlines in America.

Some of Sally's relatives began to pressure her to quickly forgive her father, come to a family reunion, and smile for a family photo. Sally tried to recover quickly from the devastating news, mistakenly thinking that was what godly submission required. But Sally was stunned, hurt, angry, and confused. Her disappointment was devastating, and she needed time to let the reality sink in. The more she tried to have enough resources to recover instantly, the more frustrated she became, and she began to realize that her attempt to force herself to forgive quickly wasn't honest. She *was* willing to forgive, but she was not ready to do all the things her family was demanding she do *immediately* as evidence of her submission and obedience to God. Finally, Sally prayed, tearfully admitting that it was God she must obey, not "men" (or family members if they are demanding what God does not). She realized that all the other musts, shoulds, ought-tos, and have-tos were the result of Sally's trusting herself to have the resources she needed instead of trusting God to supply them in his time.

Instead of demanding so much of herself, Sally started doing what she *could* do—what God *enabled* her to do. Each day she reaffirmed her faith in Christ's power and her forgiveness of her father by praying, "I choose to forgive. God, help me overcome my unforgiveness." This was something similar to what the father of the boy with an evil spirit said to Jesus: "I do believe; help me overcome my unbelief!" (Mark 9:24).

For the time being, aligning her will with God's will over and over again was all Sally could do with integrity, and that was enough to please God. Of course, she would like to have been at the end of the forgiveness process, with all her feelings settled in a peaceful place. Her family would have liked that too. But God had not yet supplied the resources for her to get to that place. As she surrendered to God *what she was able* to surrender and trusted that what God gave her would be enough, Sally gradually found peace in the process of forgiveness. She was also able to give up resentment toward her family for pressuring her, because she knew God was not the one expecting her to have emotional resources he had not yet given her.

Jesus Invites Us to Submit

Sometimes we get the idea that it's our job to pressure others until they submit to God. But this isn't God's way of gaining our submission. It only forces the issue by imposing our will on others. If we're trying to force submission, we're still hooked into the myth and violating the freedom Christ wants us to have in willingly choosing his way. Henri Nouwen wrote, "If we were forced to love Jesus and to respond to him only as he ordered, we would not really be lovers."[1] Instead of forcing, God *invites* us to do things his way because he wants our love and willing obedience and he wants to bless us, his children.

When we catch ourselves desperately wanting others to do things our way (or if we are under the thumbs of people who want us to do it their way), we need to remember that God has given each person the ability to think, weigh options, develop discernment, heal, grow, and make choices. He hasn't assigned any of us the duty of making that happen in someone else. Instead, he simply asks, "Will you submit yourself to me?"

In *The Man Who Listens to Horses*, Monty Roberts teaches readers about the nature of submission. Monty grew up on a ranch with his father, who broke horses the traditional way, through the use of dominance and whippings. Monty's father had beaten him as well. As years passed and Monty watched his father beat horses into submission so that they would accept a rider, he knew there must be a better way to get a horse's cooperation.

> "If we were forced to love Jesus and to respond to him only as he ordered, we would not really be lovers."
> —Henri Nouwen

Monty began to observe how the animals behaved and related to each other. He noticed the way the dominant mare in the group cocked her ear, lowered her head, and turned her body slightly to invite another horse to come into the group. Monty called this behavior "join up." Later he found great success in training horses by gaining their trust and by letting his behavior ask, "Will you?" instead of demand, "You must."[2]

Our friend Sally also "joined up" with Christ, finding hope and grace to persevere. She shows us a unique glimpse of Christ as she steels herself in God's presence and in his truth and keeps things simple. As Jesus tenderly asks, "Will you?" day by day instead of demanding "You will," Sally is taking little steps on the path God shows her.

Jesus Makes Our Resources "Enough"

> Taking the five loaves and the two fish and looking up to heaven, [Jesus] gave thanks and broke them. Then he gave them to the disciples to set before the people. They all ate and were satisfied, and the disciples picked up twelve basketfuls of broken pieces that were left over.
>
> LUKE 9:16-17

It was two weeks before Christmas, just after my divorce. The holiday energy I'd always had in abundance in years past was totally absent. Baking cookies was drudgery. Dragging out the Christmas tree and stringing the lights for the first time as a single parent brought a lump to my throat and a hollow ache to the pit of my stomach. As my sons and I went through the motions of holiday decorating, I turned my head away often, hoping they wouldn't see my tears.

Not only was my emotional tank empty but my bank account was also bone dry.

What can I give my kids for Christmas this year, Lord? How will Scott and Brent buy a present for their dad and each other? What will we eat for our holiday dinner, and who will eat with us? Of course, there was no audible answer to my tearful inquisition.

The next weekend at church, Brent's Sunday school teacher handed me a Christmas card and said, "Merry Christmas to you and the boys!" I thanked him and tucked the card into my Bible, waiting until we got home to open it. To my utter amazement, inside the card, wrapped in a lavender tissue, were eight one-hundred-dollar bills! Eight hundred dollars? *This is incredible! Lord, this is way more than enough!*

I immediately called a family meeting, and my sons and I sat down on the living-room floor. I lit a candle to signify that I was about to announce something really special. After I told Scott and Brent the news, we thanked God together for this happy, undeserved surprise. Of course, their Christmas lists instantly grew quite long as they rattled off their requests, now that we had some money.

I treasure that memory of how God provided so lovingly for us that year through kind and generous Christian friends when we were at the end of our resources. Many things were going wrong—I was facing surgery, and the washing machine and car had broken down. But in this time of immense emptiness, God filled us full with his many blessings—not just money, car repairs, and an invitation to Christmas dinner—but also Christ's tender, reassuring presence. At a time when I couldn't scrape anything off the bottom of my resource bowl, God came to us and made sure we had more than enough.

Something about such times almost makes me long for impoverishment—but not quite. I'm human enough to enjoy having food in the pantry, a working washing machine, and not being in the red financially. Still, it's nice to have those memories of what happened once when I thought I had nothing to feed my kids but God had other ideas.

If *I* Were in Charge . . .

Discovering our emptiness seems like a bad thing, especially if we like to give and minister to others. But our emptiness can cause us to give ourselves to God more completely and trust him more fully in the midst of our problems. We are his, and he will supply all that we need to do what he wants us to do. We learn this in different ways throughout our lives when our jars are empty of all kinds of resources: time, energy, money, or emotional well-being.

I'll never forget the first time I met Marianne. I recall being refreshed by her winsome spirit and genuine smile. Although Marianne and her family lived in the same Dallas suburb Frank and I lived in at the time, she had somehow learned to live peacefully in the midst of the hectic pace of city life.

I once asked Marianne how she had managed to attain a genuinely peaceful spirit in the midst of their family's trials. Their two daughters had been molested by a member of their extended family when the girls were small. At the time, Marianne responded by trying her best to protect the girls, homeschooling them through high school and closely supervising all their activities.

"God's sovereignty is the only thing big enough to bring peace to my soul," said Marianne. I was puzzled. Here was a woman with every right to hold a grudge against God for letting her down, if ever a person had such a right. But Marianne went on to explain. "Looking back, I now see that all along, I actually thought I could protect my daughters myself. If I could only be careful enough, I could create the safety they needed."

With the help of a trusted counselor, her daughters had worked through the trauma of the abuse. Then, while away at college, the older daughter was raped.

"When Ginny was raped," Marianne said, "I felt as though God had allowed her femininity to be totally stomped on, spat upon, and walked away from. I saw only pain and destruction in my daughter's future." Marianne had found that no matter how hard she tried, she could not protect her daughters, even from life's worst traumas. Her resources were not adequate after all.

"But it seems that would make you *doubt* God's sovereignty," I probed. "How did this realization help you trust him?"

"One day I was standing in the shower, and I became intensely aware of my hatred for Ginny's abuser," said Marianne.

"Hatred?" I asked.

"You better believe it—pure hate." Marianne paused a moment, then continued. "I couldn't hold in my anger any longer. I raged at God, shouting, 'I turn my back for just one moment, and look what happens! Is this how you care for my children? And I'm supposed to trust in your sovereignty?'

"But as I stood there shouting at God, I began to sense his presence. A question came to mind, as if God were asking it of me: *If you were in charge instead of me, Marianne, what would you have me do to him?*

"I screamed, 'If it were up to me, his eyes would be clawed out, and huge hunks of flesh would fall off his body! That's what would happen if I were in charge!'"

But as Marianne recited her vengeful wishes to God, an image of the boy who had abused Ginny came to her mind. "It was as if I saw his body the way I described it—with large hunks of flesh just hanging off his bones. As I stared at the boy's body, it slowly transformed into an image of Jesus."

Marianne went on to say that this was God's way of reminding her that Jesus had already taken all the angry lashings, gashes, and bruises she wanted to inflict on the abuser. Jesus had already absorbed all of them into his own body. Furthermore, Jesus had taken those marks of hatred and revenge and borne them not only for the boy but also for Marianne.

My friend's eyes glistened as she concluded the story about that day in the shower and how a horrifying experience had not only confirmed God's merciful love for all people but had reminded her of how fortunate it is for all of us that *God* is the One in charge—not us. Because he is sovereign—and we are not—we are free of burdensome decisions about how to mete out justice to others. While Marianne had once expected God to protect her family from tragedy and it appeared he hadn't, the sovereign mercy of Christ eventually empowered both her and her daughter to look upon the abuser with compassion and humility. But that happened on God's terms—not on Marianne's.

When we submit to God's sovereignty, we will not be disappointed. It may seem as if we don't have the resources we need to entrust our lives to God, especially when tragedy strikes. It may seem that we don't have anything left. But God says he will make sure we have enough. Submitting to God's oversight and giving ourselves and our loved ones to him in honest prayer leads to freedom. It also develops perseverance, because it takes persistence to practice this kind of submission. When we turn to him, he takes us just as we are and leads us to a place beyond ourselves—so that we can freely serve others in his name.

The Freedom of Belonging to God

> You are not your own; you were bought at a price.
> 1 CORINTHIANS 6:19-20

Before Frank and I moved into the historic district of McKinney, Texas, we used to drive through the neighborhood and admire the century-old houses and mature trees and dream of owning one of the old Victorian homes. But most of the homes in our price range were in need of major restoration, and we'd already burned out on a lot of do-it-yourself projects in a previous home.

Then one day we detoured down a side street and saw a For Sale sign in front of a smaller Victorian that looked to be in pretty good shape. On a lark we decided to take a look at the inside of the house. The Realtor accommodated, and the minute we walked inside, Frank's eyes mirrored my own enchantment. The rooms were small, but we discussed how easy it would be to enlarge the living room by building onto the side of the house.

There were front and back porches where we could enjoy the trees and birds, and the picket fence surrounding the backyard let us gaze past the neighbor's clothesline and through several yards down the block. The yard also looked like a paradise for our dog, Molly, and we decided to buy the place.

The day we moved in, the Realtor gave us a history book that came with the house and contained photos of all the restoration work that had been done since the house was built in 1891. We sat on the front porch and read the names of all the people who had lived in the house, and we realized our names would go into the book too.

Neighbors came to welcome us. People walking their dogs stopped to talk. We met people whose grandparents had once lived in the house and heard stories of things that had happened there over the years. We even learned that it was once called "Bowen's Beanery" because a Mrs. Bowen cooked beans for workers who boarded in its bedrooms.

Frank and I started to realize that this house was not our house—that we would never own it, even if we paid off the mortgage. It had its own life and stories to tell. It had been around longer than either of us, and we were just a couple of people moving through. It really belonged to McKinney's history—not to us—and it always would.

Strangely, knowing we could never really own the place endeared it to us even more. The living room began to feel cozy instead of small. We rubbed lemon oil on the wooden mantel surrounding the little brick fireplace and made plans to resurface and polish the old claw-foot tub that stood under a round stained-glass window in the bathroom. We were here today, but someday we would be gone.

Our house reminds us of the freedom we have in Christ *because we don't own ourselves*. We are his! He has bought us at a great price, and we are just wayfarers passing through this life on earth. Heaven is our real home. When we remember that it is God who owns us and all that he gives us, we give to others generously, freely, and abandon ourselves to his care instead of placing unrealistic demands on ourselves. We don't really own anything—not our homes or our children or our own lives. Everything is all on loan to us as gifts of his grace, and only for one day at a time.

Sometimes it may feel as if God is asking more of us than we have to give, the way the widow at Zarephath must have felt when Elijah told her to bake him a cake with the last of her flour and oil. But if only we can remember that God, who owns us, has resources beyond those we can see, we will be able to offer up what we have, in gratitude. We will be able to trust him to multiply what we give to him and turn it into enough or even more than enough. We will be able to live in the freedom of *not* owning ourselves—the freedom of being Christ's servants.

> *Thy servant, Lord, hath nothing in the house,*
> *Not even one small pot of common oil;*
> *For he who never cometh but to spoil*
> *Hath raided my poor house again, again,*
> *That ruthless strong man armed, whom men call Pain.*
>
> *I thought that I had courage in the house,*
> *And patience to be quiet and endure,*
> *And sometimes happy songs; not I am sure*
> *Thy servant truly hath not anything,*
> *And see, my song-bird hath a broken wing.*

My servant, I have come into the house—
I, who know Pain's extremity so well
That there can never be the need to tell
His power to make the flesh and spirit quail;
Have I not felt the scourge, the thorn, the nail?

And I, his Conqueror, am in the house,
Let not your heart be troubled; do not fear;
Why shouldst thou, child of Mine, if I am here?
My touch will heal thy song-bird's broken wing,
And he shall have a braver song to sing.

—Amy Carmichael[3]

● ● ● ● ● ● ● ● ● ● ● ●

REFLECT ON THE TRUTH

The following questions and exercises are intended to help you prayerfully reflect on what you have read. You might want to use a notebook or journal for writing down your thoughts, feelings, and prayers as you go along.

Giving of Ourselves Brings Freedom

1. Open with prayer.

2. Read Ephesians 2:10: "We are God's workmanship, created in Christ Jesus to do good works, which God prepared in advance for us to do." Reflect and write down your thoughts about the freedom that comes from knowing that we are God's workmanship—not our own.

3. Write a prayer expressing the freedom of not owning yourself or those you love or things you have in this life. Here is a sample prayer to help you get started:

Lord Jesus, I am just traveling through this world. This is not my home. The things I often think are so bad—when I lose what I wanted so badly or someone misunderstands my attempt at kindness—are just evidence that I do not belong here. Help me every day to remember this, Jesus: *I am yours.* My loved ones, children, family and friends, my house, the dog, the trees on our street—all of these are yours. My time is yours. When I feel pressured, remind me of this. Thank you for all the blessings you allow me to enjoy during my stay here. Thank you for making me a little stronger today and for making me *your* workmanship and not my own.

Be creative, and let gratitude bubble up from the depths of your heart. Save your prayer so that you can look back later and see the ways God has faithfully strengthened you and made you more and more *his.*

4. Close in prayer, ending with the prayer of surrender: "Lord, thank you for loving and accepting me. I turn over to you my heart, mind, body, and soul. All that I am belongs to you, through Christ, who loved me and gave himself for me. Amen."

TAKE THE TRUTH WITH YOU

I am God's workmanship—a work in progress. I will freely submit my life to God, and although I am unworthy of his blessing, I will trust him to supply all that I need to follow him.

11

Dying to Self in Community

Christian community is the place where we keep the flame of hope alive among us and take it seriously, so that it can grow and become stronger in us. —Henri Nouwen[1]

THE MYTH: Biblical submission requires that we inspire others with our unity and perfection so that they will want to be Christians too.

A few years ago at the Seattle Special Olympics, nine contestants, all physically or mentally disabled, assembled at the starting line for the 100-yard dash. At the gun, they all started out, not exactly in a dash but with relish, to run the race, to the finish, and win. All, that is, except one little boy who stumbled on the asphalt, tumbled over, and began to cry. The other eight heard the boy cry. They slowed down and looked back. Then they all turned around and went back. Every one of them. One girl with Down syndrome bent down and kissed him and said, "This will make it

165

better." Then all nine linked arms and walked together to the finish line. Everyone in the stadium stood and cheered; the cheering went on for several minutes. People who were there are still telling the story.[2]

When I read this story, I was deeply touched. I read it to my husband and some friends, who were also impressed by the compassion and unity of spirit among these children at the Special Olympics. I even shared the story at a women's retreat. Then one day I decided to tell the story in more detail, so I looked it up to get more information. What I found was that although the story was mostly true, it was not altogether true.

According to the Special Olympics Washington office, this incident happened at a 1976 track-and-field event in Spokane, Washington. A contestant did fall at the beginning of the race, and one or two athletes turned back to help. The other runners continued on and finished the race. The one or two who turned back to help the stumbling runner did cross the finish line with him. As it turned out, the story had been embellished because that version would be more inspirational.[3]

This reveals an important lesson about humanity: We all long for a bond of unity with others, a bond that goes beyond competition, stops and reaches out to those who struggle along the way, and cares enough to help them become winners. Yet we seem to feel a greater need to preserve inspirational value than to preserve the truth.

The body of Christ can become overly focused on inspiring others, too. Sometimes we try to appear so alike in our beliefs and opinions within the church because we think that means we have achieved unity. Of course, we need to find a fellowship of believers we can grow with, enjoy, and feel close to, but sometimes we get things turned around and think it's not enough to simply approach God together for worship, prayer, and study. We want those outside the church to see that we have achieved sanctification so that they will want to be *like us*. But that's not what sanctification and dying to self in a community of believers are about.

In our efforts to inspire those outside the church, we may embellish what goes on in our churches and our relationships as Christians. The world looks on and laughs, already knowing when we're not being authentic, but we're afraid to admit that although we belong to Christ, we're really not all that together, we're really quite handicapped, and we stumble, just like everyone else.

The truth is, none of us would make it to the finish line if God's merciful hands weren't reaching out to us from the other side and drawing us onward. When we insist on clinging to our pretense about who we are as the church instead of admitting our utter dependence on the One who draws us homeward, we miss our best opportunities to share God's love with those who have stumbled. We pass by the hurting, doubting, floundering ones falling at the sidelines because we're afraid the unembellished truth is not inspiring enough. Yet from birth to death, Christ's heart was never set on impressing, or even inspiring, people. Jesus simply trusted and obeyed his Father, and he always told the truth.

> *When we insist on clinging to our pretense about who we are as the church instead of admitting our utter dependence on the One who draws us homeward, we miss our best opportunities to share God's love with those who have stumbled.*

As the church, we're often uncomfortable saying to the world, "All we've got here is Jesus. Are you interested in joining us?" But authentic biblical submission asks that we remain transparent about our imperfections and that we live truthfully and humbly in service to God and others. As we do, the Holy Spirit reveals Christ in us and inspires others to become *like him*. This is the foundation of authentic community life in which the ministry of the Holy Spirit is active. This is true unity, and Satan does all he can to trick us, distract us, disillusion us, and keep us from lifting up Jesus Christ and him only in both our personal lives and our communities. Fortunately, Christ is able to keep us on track and in step.

Christ Keeps Us in Step in Community

As I was reading Ephesians in *The Message* one day, the apostle Paul shed some light on my confusion about our behavior within the body of Christ and how it affects the world around us. Paul reminds Christians of the immense mercy and love with which Christ once embraced each of their sin-dead souls: "It's God's gift from start to finish! We don't play the major role. If we did, we'd probably go around bragging that we'd done the whole thing!" (2:8-9).

Paul then cautions the Ephesians not to take this lavish gift for granted but to do something worthwhile with it: "Here's what I want you to do. . . . I want you to get out there and walk— better yet, run!—on the road God called you to travel. . . . You were all called to travel on the same road and in the same direction, so stay together, both outwardly and inwardly. . . . Everything you are and think and do is permeated with Oneness. But that doesn't mean you should all look and speak and act the same. Out of the generosity of Christ, each of us is given his own gift" (4:1-7).

I closed my eyes and mused on what Paul's description of unity in the body of Christ might look like: *All of us going in the same direction, staying together in the same pack, and being grateful for our differences.* I kept reading.

"No prolonged infancies among us, please. . . . God wants us to grow up, to know the whole truth and tell it in love—like Christ in everything. We take our lead from Christ, who is the source of everything we do. He keeps us in step with each other. His very breath and blood flow through us, nourishing us so that we will grow up healthy in God, robust in love" (4:14-16).

As I came to the end of that section of Ephesians, I took a moment to let the words sink into my heart so the Holy Spirit could teach me: As we realize how often we have fallen short of God's standard, how many times we have fallen down, yet how lovingly and mercifully Christ has lifted us to our feet again and again, it's much easier to accept others who also fall short of God's standard. It is he—not us—who keeps us in step, and staying in step doesn't mean being alike. We each take our lead from him. Just as we have many imperfections as individuals, so does the church.

How different these thoughts were from the competitive games I once engaged in with other Christians. Perhaps you have done that too. But having found liberty in Christ, we are able to lay aside power plays, control, manipulation, and the endless quest for accomplishment and embellishment in the church. Instead, we grow to respect others, and at the same time we respect ourselves *in appreciation and gratitude for our differences*. We see that God is glorified in our differences. We see that he keeps us in step with his other children who are different from us.

When we come to church in an attitude of mutual respect and love, knowing that only God can be God, we are bound together in peace, gratitude, humility, and unity of Spirit. The church becomes a safe, welcoming place where broken, scared, and lonely people can come together and find healing because of the love of Jesus.

You may be thinking, *Wait a minute. I've read that passage in Ephesians 4. I know that's the goal and that's the way church is supposed to be, but that's not the way church has been for me.*

Okay. Let's agree that the *goal* is to grow to maturity in Christ, to appreciate our various gifts, and to stay together as we run toward the finish line. But let's be truthful about the fact that we have handicaps, habits, and limitations that annoy and grate on each other. We have different opinions about the way God relates to people, different views about how to interpret certain passages of Scripture. We have conflict among church board members that would try the patience of the world's most saintly people. Some Christians have suffered wounds inflicted by those within the walls of churches and been left spiritually battered, crying on the asphalt, and nobody has come to lift them up, dust them off, and help them along. How are these people supposed to stay with the pack and keep going? How do the wounded become strengthened so that they can die to themselves for Christ's glory? How can you and I pitch in and cooperate with God's overall plan, especially with people who are so different from us and may have had life experiences totally foreign to us even though we're all Christians? For one thing, we can acknowledge and respect our diversity in the body of Christ.

Same Track, Different Track Records

> Though I am free from all men, I have made myself a servant to all, *that I might win the more.*
> 1 CORINTHIANS 9:19, NKJV (emphasis added)

If we were to think of the Christian life as a hundred-yard dash, we would assume that we all lined up on the same starting line, the same point on the racetrack. But this assumption would be false. Our life in Christ starts when we take Jesus as our Savior. But before that happens, our life's track has already led us through experiences that have greatly affected us as women.

Some of us were born into more chaos than others. Some were close to their moms and dads growing up. Others were physically

170

or sexually abused. Some were encouraged to pursue their interests and talents as they grew and matured. Others were demeaned or criticized for being overweight or too short or too tall, or were cursed at by people they should have been able to trust. None of us had perfect parents or role models. We all have somewhat tainted impressions of the God who stands eagerly waiting for us at the end of our race. But *all* of God's children who ever lined up to live for Christ by taking him as their Savior—*all*—are blessed, not cursed.

It's easy for some Christians to believe this. It is *incredibly difficult* for others. We have different handicaps and limitations, and we run at different speeds. (It's good to keep in mind as you look at the faces of women in church on a Sunday morning that you have no idea where their track might have taken them before they got there or what it took for some of them just to show up.) Unless we embrace our blessing as a child of God—*no matter what trials we've endured*—our wounds will continually rise up and defeat us by keeping us focused on our own pain.

But what really matters is that each of us runs life's race for Christ's glory. If this is our highest aim and we are running under the authority of the Holy Spirit and the Scriptures, we will help others live for his glory too. This is the work of the Holy Spirit, who shines through our lives even when they are quite unimpressive.

If you have been wounded within the body of Christ, God did not intend for you to be hurt, confused, or betrayed there. All of God's people, including church authorities, will have to answer to him for the way they have treated his children in his house. But God's purposes go beyond your wounds. As you continue on your Christian growth journey, you may need to adjust your expectations of pastors and church leaders so that you don't see them as being on spiritual pedestals. Be a part of a safe, healthy church community—don't expect it to be perfect!—where people worship, pray, think, study the Bible, find friends, find family, ask questions, and have opinions and feelings. If you have experienced unhealthy relationships in the body of Christ, ask yourself, *How has God used these experiences and people to help me grow? Do I need healing from God?*

Although healing takes time, Romans 8:28 is true and operative, even when it comes to wounds received within the body of Christ: "In all things God works for the good of those who love him." As we persevere, our suffering allows us to identify more with the sufferings of Christ. This is one way God fleshes out the truth that his "power is made perfect in [our] weakness" (2 Corinthians 12:9).

You may have enjoyed years of positive and loving experience in the church. You may not have endured many problems in relationships or life circumstances. You may even feel a twinge of guilt at the thought that others are hurting emotionally or enduring difficult trials while you have received the kinds of blessings many pray for but do not get. Don't take on false guilt because you have been blessed with healthy relationships, good physical health, or financial resources. Rather, rejoice because you are a light for others, a witness of Christ's grace in giving you those things.

If you have been the recipient of these blessings, keep letting Jesus shine through you. But be aware that among many Christians disillusionment with the church is a very real problem. In chapter 4 I described wounds I experienced from Christians within the church. When Frank and I left that small legalistic church, we were so disillusioned and confused that for a while it seemed we might never set foot in a church again.

We had no idea then that God would use this experience to strengthen us and help us to grow and mature as Christians. At the time we knew only that we needed an extended time-out from church—time to clear our heads. We needed time to separate our concept of who God is, as revealed in the Bible and by the Holy Spirit, from the distorted view of him that had come to us through those who had a mistaken perception of him. I am not saying that staying out of church was the best choice we could have made. But at the time, it was the only thing we knew to do in order to give our souls a rest. After several months of clearing our heads and renewing our knowledge of the character of God as we read the Scriptures (mostly the Psalms), we began once again to venture out to church.

At first, we sat in the back pews anonymously, letting the words of sermons float over our heads, listening to the voices of others singing hymns, and wondering if we would ever again find a fit in the body of Christ. We were careful to look for characteristics of truth, well-being, and health in a church body. We looked for acceptance and mutual respect among the people. We looked for wisdom and truth telling in the leadership. We gave up our illusions of finding perfection in the church, just as we'd given up the illusion of perfection for ourselves.

After attending a couple of churches and maintaining only minimal involvement, Frank and I felt it was time to settle into a church in our own town, perhaps even in our own neighborhood. Months had passed, and God had done a lot of healing in our hearts through Christian counseling, friends, neighbors, and family members. We had grown up a lot, but we still didn't know where we belonged.

Where do we go, Lord? we asked. We began to sense a connection with many of the people in the churches we visited. We heard words of truth coming from their pulpits, and we felt connected to the people in our neighborhood as well. After a lot of looking, we realized that God had set our hearts right about how the church was to be and that was far more important than sitting inside the right church. This didn't happen overnight, and it involved spending time in churches that were safe, though, of course, imperfect. Beyond that, all we did was accept the hand of friendship extended to us by so many kind people. In time we settled into a small church near our neighborhood.

Looking back over my life, I see that ironically, I learned many of my deepest spiritual lessons in the church—through both positive and negative examples. I learned what God is like and what he is *not* like. My confusion about God's character forced me to examine my own thinking and to identify ways flawed human authority figures had contributed to my distorted view of my heavenly Father.

God didn't stop his work in my life. I was learning what it really means to die to self, both as a woman and as part of a Christian community, to risk the rejection of people as I stood secure in the love of God. Through community experiences, both positive and negative, Christ was gradually healing and strengthening me in my inner woman.

In what ways is he strengthening your character, perhaps through both positive and negative experiences in church, at work, or in your family? Unless you take time to reflect on this, you can miss seeing how God is cultivating holiness in your life. He always does it in his own way, often by rubbing us up against people who are different and who have different opinions from ours. It's all part of his plan to ready us for his Kingdom.

God Heals through Community

> Mostly what God does is love you. Keep company
> with him and learn a life of love.

EPHESIANS 5:2, *THE MESSAGE*

The 1996 film *Shine* gives us a glimpse of the healing power of love and acceptance within community, even when wounds are very deep. David Helfgott is a child prodigy whose over-bearing father beats him for wanting to rise to his potential as a musician.

David escapes his father's emotional and physical abuse by winning an invitation to attend a university in London. But the wounds of his childhood, along with the pressure of having to do well in his music program, force David to the breaking point, and he suffers a breakdown during a performance.

After a lengthy stay in an institution, David, now an adult, is released and begins to find his way in society. His rapid-cycling thoughts and repetitive speech patterns make it difficult for others to be around him. On the other hand, the warmth and friendliness that have always been a part of David find their way to the surface, and he begins to rise above the handicap of his schizophrenia. He makes friends. People put up with his messi-ness, his absentmindedness. They love having him around because he's just, well—David.

David meets Gillian, who sees beyond his handicap and limita-tions and into his heart. With her support David prepares for and plays a concert. At the end the audience's loud applause brings tears to David's eyes. He has not only survived but also lived to the very best of his ability because he has found a healing community of people who love and accept him just for being David.

Is this what you experience in your church today? If so, keep spreading the truth and love of Christ in that community and beyond the walls of your church. If not, think about what it would be like in the church today if we were more like the community who nourished David's spirit until it thrived. What would it take in our churches for us to provide a safe place where we could sit in our Bible study groups and be real with one another? What would it be like if we took seriously these words

175

written to the Christians at Rome: "Let's just go ahead and be what we were made to be, without enviously or pridefully comparing ourselves with each other, or trying to be something we aren't" (Romans 12:3-5, *The Message*).

Where do the confidence and inner peace come from to get beyond comparisons, pride, and pretense when we are together at church? They are the result of being sure of God's love and acceptance so that we can let others see us as we really are—limitations, handicaps, and all—and let the light of God's trans-forming power shine through us. This is exactly what the evil one does *not* want. That's why he's attacking our churches today, turning us against one another, discouraging, tricking, and deceiving us, luring us off track so we won't unite and fight against evil as the body of Christ. Whether you are among the walking wounded or are a resilient Christian soldier, if your heart longs to die to self and serve God and others sacrificially, be warned that even with the help of wisdom and discernment, there's a risk involved and sometimes a price to be paid for telling the truth and being real.

The evil one does not even want us to dream about what it might look like to lift up Jesus and him only. We often memorize Jesus' words in the last part of John 10:10: "I have come that they may have life, and have it to the full." But the first half of the verse says, "The thief comes only to steal and kill and destroy." We need to remember that we are Christian soldiers on a common mission, and our enemy is the evil one—not each other. When we forgive others for misunderstanding us, taking advantage of us, or even persecuting us, it's a victory for good and a defeat for evil. When we persevere in working out a conflict and show respect for those who differ from us, we glorify Christ.

Our diversity makes us stronger as a community because we have to work hard to arrive at solutions instead of getting things our way every time. With each victory for Christ, we die to self a little more. Our maturing relationships with other Christians become a precious gift—a fruit of God's transforming love.

Dying to Self as a Church

If you have ever had a broken bone, you probably know that the mended part is stronger than it was before the bone was broken. This principle applies to other areas in which we have been broken as well. Through God's healing grace and over time, we become stronger in the areas in which we were broken. As we die to our desire to nurse our hurts in bitterness, we begin to discover that even Christians who have wounded us deeply have contributed to our growth. God's redeeming love uses even our offenders as his instruments in the process of strengthening us and making us holy. Sometimes we even have the opportunity (when God supplies the resources and ability!) to contribute to our offenders' healing.

I am not suggesting that you seek out these offenders or go looking for unresolved trouble—it will find you. But because of the depth of God's love for you, nothing is beyond the realm of what he can use to make you more his. God can bring us to a place of gratitude for every experience as we keep pressing toward the mark for Christ's glory, continue to learn new lessons, become wiser, and ask Christ to shine through our brokenness so that others will see him living in us.

God turns weakness into strength and builds skills from what was once devastation, for the benefit of others and ultimately for his glory. As Christians, we're *all* on our way to dying to self for Christ's glory, and he continually offers each of us opportunities to die, because the truth is, there is not one group of people who are always wounded and another group of people who are always well. In our war against the evil one, we take turns serving on the front lines. We take turns being wounded, needing our emotions bandaged, and finding healing. But we can't see the "bandages" on others or guess who may recently have been run through with news that their child has cancer or that someone's husband has left her for another woman unless we learn to be vulnerable with each other as we come together at church.

If the church is to be effective in extending the love of Christ to those who enter in search of sanctuary, we must learn to meet the *real* needs of people. We must put the needs of others ahead of our own complacency and comfort as we sit in the same pew Sunday after Sunday. We need to welcome people as they are and help them feel at ease among us. But where do we start?

We start by listening and accepting them—listening to hear, not to change, fix, or judge. We resist the impulse to tell them what they should do or to tell them to "just trust in the Lord," even if we think we know what God would have them do. We resist the impulse to judge them or to tell them to have faith or to think positively because we really have no understanding of their internal and external resources—only God does. We *do* come alongside them, worship the Lord, and seek his guidance, comfort, and joy. Whether we sing contemporary choruses and pray spontaneous prayers, sing traditional hymns and recite the Apostles' Creed, or proceed through liturgy and sacraments, something supernatural happens when we come humbly into God's presence together: We realize that God knows each of us intimately and that we are all precious in his sight. Only when we get beyond fixing, judging, competing, and envying are we free to lift each other up as Christ has lifted each of us up so many times. "Christ within us" is strengthened in our community, and we begin to bear some hint of resemblance to the community of the Trinity, which is our only worthy model.

The Unembellished Truth about Community

At a conference in Dallas a couple of years ago, Richard Foster gave a talk on "Transforming Grace." He had this to say about the holy community of the Trinity:

> In the Trinity, there is no competition. While people today get all caught up in debates, trying to understand who's more important [Father, Son, or Holy Spirit], there is no subordination in the Trinity, because They will have nothing of it. The Father says, "Look to the Son." The Son says, "Look to the Spirit." The Spirit says, "Look to the Father." . . . And on and on it goes, as a glorious community of loving Persons simply love to lift each other up, for the glory of God.[4]

This is the standard for our relationships in the body of Christ, and this is the only inspirational story about community worth telling, retelling, or modeling our churches after. It is also the model of community the world needs to see demonstrated. We who know Christ's love become his Olympians, running with the flame of his love, which dwells among us, lifting up one another when we fall, and passing the flame to others along the way.

Only when we are secure in Christ's love, strengthened in our inner woman because of his empowerment, are we content to lift up God the Father, Son, and Holy Spirit—not ourselves, our church, or even our faith—but Christ only. When we deeply know that all we really have to offer to others is companionship on our Christian journey as we worship our Lord together, acknowledging his sovereignty over everything that is true in all of our lives, the Spirit of Christ shines brightly in us, lighting the darkest corners of this world.

I was reminded of this recently at a monthly breakfast meeting with eight or nine close Christian companions. As usual, we'd met at a local restaurant and our leader, Iris, asked us to check in with each other. This was our opportunity to share gratitudes and needs as we approached God through fellowship and prayer. I knew these dear friends had been praying for me since I injured my back almost a year ago. But today I was discouraged, worn out from the chronic pain.

"I know God wants to strengthen my trust in him," I said, "but right now I don't know if trusting him means accepting more speaking engagements for the coming year or becoming content to do less." After others also shared their joys and concerns, it was time to close our meeting and be on our way. As my friends gathered their belongings and got ready to leave, several passed by my chair (I was last to get up to leave) and put their hands on my shoulders while they softly whispered prayers. One sat down beside me and assured me of her continued prayers for God's healing and direction. As I looked into the faces of these women, I saw the love and compassion of Christ looking at me through their eyes. I felt the comfort of the Holy Spirit through the touch of their hands on my shoulders. Whether God would heal my chronic back pain immediately or let it go on for the rest of my life was known only to him. But as we affirmed our mutual trust in Christ, my spirit was lifted up, my hope renewed, and I was strengthened and encouraged to persevere on my Christian journey.

What is it in your life, at this very moment, that you need most so that you can persevere and become stronger? Is it faith? hope? agape love? No matter what it is, we find it all in Christ, and it is often demonstrated to us through fellow believers. Because of God's grace, we are allowed to participate in spreading the light within us, that is Christ himself.

I began this book by exposing some of the myths Christians fall for—counterfeit perceptions that can get us off track as we try to submit our lives to Christ and die to self. I want to end by encouraging you to live the *truth* about biblical submission and dying to self—embracing your gifts and becoming fully alive to God and his leading. Christ within us raises us above our human problems and unbiblical patterns. Christ within us becomes greater than our shortsighted judgment of humanity. Christ within us fights against evil and reaches out to the world through ordinary people like you and me.

Let us throw off everything that would lure us off track. Let us live each day offering our gifts to Christ and to others around us. Let us live wholeheartedly in submission to Jesus—until we die.

> Alive, I'm Christ's messenger; dead, I'm his bounty.
> Life versus even more life! I can't lose.
> PHILIPPIANS 1:21-22, *THE MESSAGE*

REFLECT ON THE TRUTH

The following questions and exercises are intended to help you prayerfully reflect on what you have read. You might want to use a notebook or journal for writing down your thoughts, feelings, and prayers as you go along.

The Truth about the Submissive Christian Woman

1. Open with prayer.

2. Read Ephesians 4:1-6. As Christians, we yearn for a bond that goes beyond competition and envy. What does it mean to "live a

life worthy of the calling you have received"? What does it mean to achieve "unity of the Spirit through the bond of peace"?

3. As you look back over your life, can you see signs that God has been calling you to himself? Even if/when you did not know Christ, were there people in your life who taught you about what God is like and what God is *not* like? Who were they? How old were you when you learned these things from these people? God uses both positive and negative examples to help us grow in his grace.

4. Has God drawn you closer to him through blessing and fullness? through emptiness and need? through some other means?

5. Reflect on the following "Marks of a Woman Living as Her True Self for the Glory of God":

   • She has come to know Christ as her Savior and Lord.
   • She accepts the fact that she needs ongoing cleansing and healing from God. Just as we need to brush our teeth daily to keep them clean, our spirits need cleansing from sins and wounds every day. Jesus had ongoing wounds from people around him. So will we.
   • She has spiritual energy to do something ongoing for God. It will be what he directs her to do.
   • A spiritual woman has the Holy Spirit reigning in her heart. She lives out an attitude that says, "I am not for sale."
   • She faces reality and looks to God for strength to persevere and to forgive those who damage or wound her.

Write a plan on how you can come to be the person God already knows you are—your *true self*. You will be able to do it only with God's direction and power day by day. Be sure to include what God needs to heal in you.

6. Close with prayer, ending with the prayer of surrender: "Lord, thank you for loving and accepting me. I turn over to you my heart, mind, body, and soul. All that I am belongs to you, through Christ, who loved me and gave himself for me. Amen."

TAKE THE TRUTH WITH YOU

Biblical submission asks that we humbly serve God and others in our churches and remain transparent about our imperfections and failings. As we do, the Holy Spirit reveals Christ in us and inspires others to become like him. The result is authentic Christian community. May the light of Christ shine brightly in the hearts of all his people until he comes again!

GUIDELINES FOR
SMALL GROUP DISCUSSIONS

If you decide to read and discuss the book as part of a group of women, I encourage you to cultivate an atmosphere of openness, grace, and respect for the individuality God has created in each person in the group. *Create a place of safety where women can get together and be real.*

There should be a leader, who makes sure the group follows the guidelines. Pray for one another and trust that the Holy Spirit will guide each woman. Begin your meetings with prayer. Review guidelines at your first meeting. I encourage each group member to find his or her own favorite supportive verses from the Bible in addition to those given, because that will enhance your growth journey.

To encourage openness, trust, and mutual respect, keep the comments shared in your small groups confidential. The guideline is that what's shared in the group stays in the group.

Do not give each other advice. Practice the art of listening. Listen to hear and understand, not to fix. We are often uncomfortable seeing another person in pain or distress, so our natural tendency is to pacify, offer advice, or try to relieve the pain. *Don't.* God is the fixer. You are there to listen, encourage, and offer support during the group meeting. *When we listen to others, the person sharing feels cared for and may sense God's comforting presence through the people surrounding her.*

After the group meeting, members may be drawn to further

one-on-one discussion with someone they identified with. God also works in this way to connect people. Refrain from cross-talk, that is, from doing or saying the following:

- Giving advice: "You should . . ."
- Criticizing: "You shouldn't have . . ."
- Condemning: "You shouldn't have . . ."
- Controlling: "You should . . ."
- Debating: "Wouldn't it have been better to . . ."
- Dominating: "What I think you should do is . . ."
- Giving unsolicited feedback: "You didn't ask me, but . . ."
- Interrupting: Butting in when another person is sharing or not allowing that person to finish.[1]

Give everyone who wants to share and be part of the discussion a turn. Some people may choose to pass, and that is fine. The leader should go over group guidelines (above) first, then address the questions for each group meeting. Ask who would like to respond first, and if no one volunteers, the leader should share first to break the ice. As one person speaks, the others are listening. As we listen, we are also thinking—that's part of communication. But if we interrupt the one who is sharing or try to fix that person, we are engaging in cross-talk. The group leader should gently remind the person who interrupted of the guidelines above. Close your meeting with a brief prayer by one member, ending with gratitude that no matter what state we are in right now, God loves us, and he has not yet completed his work in us.[2]

NOTES

PART 1: EXPOSING THE MYTHS

1. Teresa of Avila, quoted in David Hazard, *Majestic Is Your Name: A 40-Day Journey in the Company of Teresa of Avila* (Minneapolis, Minn.: Bethany, 1993), 32.

Chapter 1: Have You Lost Yourself?

1. Amy Tan, quoted in Sarah Ban Breathnach, *Simple Abundance: A Daybook of Comfort and Joy* (New York: Warner, 1995), March 14.
2. A. W. Tozer, *The Pursuit of God* (Harrisburg, Pa.: Christian Publications, 1948), 44.
3. Julian of Norwich, quoted in David Hazard, *I Promise You a Crown* (Minneapolis, Minn.: Bethany, 1995), 14.

Chapter 2: Do Your Choices Reflect Your Commitment?

1. Sheila Walsh, *Honestly* (Grand Rapids, Mich.: Zondervan, 1996), 62.
2. Anne Morrow Lindbergh, *Gift from the Sea* (New York: Pantheon, 1955), 26.
3. Henri Nouwen, *The Return of the Prodigal Son: A Meditation on Fathers, Brothers, and Sons* (New York: Doubleday, 1992), 71.

Chapter 3: Is Your Success Formula Failing?

1. Alfred, Lord Tennyson, "In Memoriam," *The Oxford Anthology of English Literature,* vol. 3 (New York: Oxford University Press, 1975), 865.
2. Anne Morrow Lindbergh, *Gift from the Sea* (New York: Pantheon, 1955), 26.
3. *Merriam-Webster's Collegiate Dictionary,* 10th ed., s.v. "Meek."
4. Henri Nouwen, *The Inner Voice of Love* (New York: Doubleday, 1996), 9.
5. Nouwen, *Inner Voice,* 13.

Chapter 4: Are You Crawling onto the Cross?

1. Brennan Manning, *The Ragamuffin Gospel* (Sisters, Ore.: Multnomah, 2000), 139.
2. Dallas Willard, *The Divine Conspiracy: Rediscovering Our Hidden Life in God* (San Francisco: HarperCollins, 1998), 143.
3. Richard Foster, *Celebration of Discipline: The Path to Spiritual Growth* (San Francisco: Harper and Row, 1978), 110.

187

4. Billy Graham, quoted in Eugene Peterson, *The Message,* Billy Graham Evangelistic Association special edition (Colorado Springs: Navpress, 1993), 360.

PART 2: EXCHANGING MYTHS FOR THE TRUTH

Chapter 5: The Truth Will Set You Free

1. John Eldredge, address to the American Association of Christian Counselors adapted from John Eldredge, *Waking the Dead: The Glory of a Heart Fully Alive* (Nashville: Nelson, 2003).
2. Henri Nouwen, *Reaching Out: The Three Movements of the Spiritual Life* (New York: Doubleday, 1975), 60.

Chapter 6: Truth and Consequences

1. Ken Gire, *Intense Moments with the Savior: Learning to Feel* (Grand Rapids, Mich.: Zondervan, 1994), xi.
2. Henri Nouwen, *The Return of the Prodigal Son,* Sounds True—1999 (unabridged audiocassette).
3. M. Scott Peck, *The Road Less Traveled: A New Psychology of Love, Traditional Values, and Spiritual Growth* (New York: Simon & Schuster, 1978), 294–95.
4. Simon Tugwell, *Reflections on the Beatitudes: Soundings in Christian Traditions* (Springfield, Ill.: Templegate, 1980), 58.
5. G. K. Chesterton, *Orthodoxy* (San Francisco: Ignatius Press, 1995), 167–68.

Chapter 7: The Power of Letting Go

1. Dallas Willard, *Renovation of the Heart: Putting on the Character of Christ* (Colorado Springs: NavPress, 2002), 215.
2. Shortened and paraphrased from *Celtic Daily Prayer: From the Northumbria Community* (San Francisco: HarperSanFrancisco, 2002), 524.
3. Helen Grace Lescheid, "A Time to Let Go," *Moody* (July/August 1986).
4. St. Therese of Lisieux, quoted in Simon Tugwell, *Reflections on the Beatitudes: Soundings in Christian Traditions* (Springfield, Ill.: Templegate, 1980), 41.
5. Mother Teresa, quoted in *The Anglican Digest* 45, no. 5 (2003): 14.
6. Simon Tugwell, *Reflections on the Beatitudes: Soundings in Christian Traditions* (Springfield, Ill.: Templegate, 1980), 23.

Chapter 8: Embracing Your Humanness

1. Richard Rohr, *Simplicity: The Art of Living,* trans. Peter Heinegg (New York: Crossroad, 1992), 38.
2. Helen Keller, quoted in *Light from Many Lamps,* ed. Lillian Eichler Watson (New York: Simon & Schuster, 1951), 93.
3. Richard Day, quoted in Elizabeth Skoglund, *More Than Coping* (Minneapolis, Minn.: World Wide Publications, 1979), 12–13.

4. Simon Tugwell, *Reflections on the Beatitudes: Soundings in Christian Traditions* (Springfield, Ill.: Templegate, 1980), 15.

5. Paul Tillich, *The Shaking of the Foundations* (New York: Scribner's, 1948), 161–62.

PART 3: DYING TO SELF AND BECOMING ALIVE TO GOD

1. Simon Tugwell, *Reflections on the Beatitudes: Soundings in Christian Traditions* (Springfield, Ill.: Templegate, 1980), 90.

Chapter 9: The Joy of True Submission

1. If you have been a Christian for a number of years and you are unable to enjoy a relationship with Christ that really makes a difference in your life, you may want to read *Fairy Tale Faith: Living in the Meantime When You Expected Happily Ever After* (Tyndale House, 2003). The book addresses common distortions of truth that block Christian women from intimacy in their relationships (including their relationship with God) and offers hope for moving beyond those distortions.

2. Elisabeth Elliot, *A Chance to Die: The Life and Legacy of Amy Carmichael* (Old Tappan, N.J.: Revell, 1987), 151.

3. Meister Eckhart, quoted in Simon Tugwell, *Reflections on the Beatitudes: Soundings in Christian Traditions* (Springfield, Ill.: Templegate, 1980), 80.

Chapter 10: The Freedom of Self-Giving

1. Henri Nouwen, *Finding My Way Home: Pathways to Life and the Spirit* (New York: Crossroad, 2001), 114.

2. Monty Roberts, *The Man Who Listens to Horses* (New York: Ballantine, 1998), 15.

3. Amy Carmichael, "Nothing in the House," *Toward Jerusalem* (Fort Washington, Pa.: Christian Literature Crusade, 1977), 44–45.

Chapter 11: Dying to Self in Community

1. Henri Nouwen, *Finding My Way Home: Pathways to Life and the Spirit* (New York: Crossroad, 2001), 106.

2. Taken from the Internet: www.snopes.com/glurge/special.htm.

3. Factual account verified by Special Olympics Office, Kinnewick, Washington.

4. Richard Foster, "Transforming Grace" (presentation, Christian Book Editors' conference, Dallas, Texas, 2001).

Guidelines for Small Group Discussions

1. This definition of cross-talk is commonly used by Alcoholics Anonymous and Al-Anon groups.

2. In some cases, a member of the group may need to be referred to a pastor, a mentor, or a professional counselor. Simply make that suggestion, and if asked, offer the name of a person or two who might help further. Be sure to keep the person's confidence.

About the Author

Brenda Waggoner is a
licensed counselor, a writer, and
a speaker. Her passion is to help
women fully appreciate the gifts
God has given them and to trust
God beyond the heartbreaks
and abrasions of life. Brenda's
book *Fairy Tale Faith* was
praised by *Publisher's Weekly* for
tackling difficult topics like self-
rejection, childhood wounds,
and disappointment with God.

Brenda lives with her husband, Frank, and their two dogs, Molly and
Rocky, in the historic district of McKinney, Texas. They enjoy taking
walks, riding bikes, going to garage sales, and having friends over for
back-porch fun and food. Frank and Brenda have three sons, a daughter-
in-law, and several grand-dogs.

Brenda is happy to hear from fellow travelers on the Christian journey
and always responds to letters and inquiries sent to Tyndale House
Publishers. You may also visit her Web site at
www.brendawaggoner.com.

FOR BOOKING INFORMATION, CONTACT:
Speak Up Speaker Services
1614 Edison Shores Place
Port Huron, MI 48060-3374
(810) 982-0898
E-mail: Speakupinc.@aol.com

*Enjoy these other great titles
from Tyndale House Publishers!*

Real Life.
Honest Women.
True Stories.

"Bask in the gentle wisdom of a trusted friend."
Ruth McGinnis, musician, speaker, and author

Fairy Tale Faith by Brenda Waggoner

Drawing on such beloved fairy tales as *The Princess Bride*, *The Lion King*, and *Sleeping Beauty*, Christian counselor Brenda Waggoner explores the miracle that is God's grace. Tackling issues such as self-esteem, body image, perfectionism, and loss, Waggoner helps women live gracefully in The Meantime while waiting for Happily Ever After. (ISBN 0-8423-7113-3, hardcover)

"This is the kind of woman I want to learn from!"
Kay Arthur

The Hungry Heart by Lynda Hunter Bjorklund

Everyone longs for intimacy. As Christians we know that intimacy, significance, and acceptance can be found in the arms of a loving and gracious God. Dr. Lynda Hunter Bjorklund teaches women how to get at that place with God and find the deep relationship that comes from really knowing the One who created you. (ISBN 0-8423-7938-X, softcover)

"Witty, acerbic, and genuinely entertaining!"
Publishers Weekly

Scandalous Grace by Julie Ann Barnhill

Scandalous Grace is the *zing* of encouragement every woman needs to transform her thoughts about herself . . . and change her relationships for the good. With gutsy honesty and stories that will have you "laughing so hard you'll snort," Julie Barnhill reveals how you can live day by day in the knowledge of God's unconditional love in the midst of "loose ends."
(ISBN 0-8423-8297-6, softcover)

Radical Forgiveness by Julie Ann Barnhill

What does it mean to *really* forgive those who have hurt you? to forgive yourself for the dumb things you've done? to forgive God for what he has—or hasn't—done? In this heartfelt, laugh-out-loud follow-up to *Scandalous Grace*, Julie Barnhill shares the life-changing power of Jesus' sacrifice on the cross and helps readers transform their thoughts and relationships for *good!*
(ISBN 1-4143-0031-X, softcover)

"Today's Christian woman should be proud to be termed a 'SHE.'"
Publishers Weekly

SHE by Rebecca St. James and Lynda Hunter Bjorklund

Today's media bombard women with messages that say, "You must be beautiful, thin, sexy, successful, strong, outgoing, and independent." But who does *God* say a woman should be? Get up close and personal with Rebecca St. James and Lynda Hunter Bjorklund as they expose the lies that drive women to distraction. As they share their own struggles, heartaches, and successes, they also reveal the truth about God's plan for women's lives. (ISBN 1-4143-0026-3, softcover)

Available wherever Christian books are sold!

Discover
FRANCINE RIVERS
all over again

"Wow is really all I can say after staying up ALL night to finish the last 300 pages of this book. . . . I cried for 30 minutes after finishing the book from sheer joy. . . . I praise God that I had the opportunity to read this book."

　　　—a reader in Lincoln, Neb.

This new edition of a Francine Rivers classic is available at a bookstore near you. Now with a free discussion guide!

Visit www.tyndale.com

Her tragic loss. His terrible secret.
And the triumph of hope.

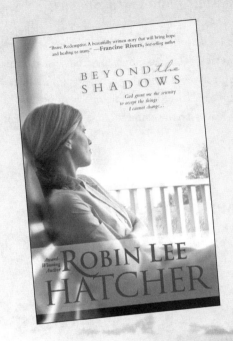

"Brave.
Redemptive.
A beautifully
written story
that brings
hope to many."

FRANCINE RIVERS

Beyond the Shadows

From her heart . . . to yours.

The gripping story of a woman in the depths
of darkness and despair—until she finds the
hope to sustain her beyond the shadows.

Available now at a bookstore near you.
www.tyndalefiction.com
www.robinleehatcher.com

The **Best-Selling**
REDEMPTION
SERIES
by Karen Kingsbury and Gary Smalley

Novelist Karen Kingsbury and relationship expert Gary Smalley team up to bring you the **Redemption series,** which explores the relationship principles Gary has been teaching for more than thirty years and applies them to one family in particular, the Baxters. In the crucible of their tragedies and triumphs, the Baxter family learns about commitment, forgiveness, faith, and the redeeming hand of God.

REDEMPTION
a story of love at all costs

REMEMBER
a journey from tragedy to healing

RETURN
a story of tenacious love
and longing for a lost son

REJOICE
a story of unspeakable loss and
the overwhelming miracle of new life

REUNION
a story of God's grace and redemption,
his victory even in the most difficult times.